MAGGS'S RAILWAY
CURIOSITIES

MAGGS'S RAILWAY CURIOSITIES

Colin Maggs

AMBERLEY

All images courtesy of the author.

First published 2016

Amberley Publishing
The Hill, Stroud
Gloucestershire, GL5 4EP

www.amberleybooks.com

British Library Cataloguing in Publication Data.
A catalogue record for this book is available from the British Library.

ISBN 978 1 4456 5265 8 (paperback)
ISBN 978 1 4456 5266 5 (ebook)

Typesetting and Origination by Amberley Publishing.
Printed in Great Britain.

Contents

1

Locomotives

Appearance

Patrick Stirling of the Glasgow & South Western Railway preferred to see a single-wheeler rather than a coupled engine at the head of his expresses, once remarking that a coupled engine at high speed reminded him of 'a laddie runnin' wi' his breeks down'. When asked by William Stroudley why he did not go in for domed boilers, his reply was to the effect that he would not tolerate anything resembling a chamber pot on his engines.

Trying It Out

One evening when Nigel Gresley had been considering corridor tenders to enable locomotive crews to swap over on a long run, one of his daughters found him on all fours, squeezing his great bulk through the narrow space formed between a wall and a row of chairs. He remarked that if he could get through, so could his biggest engineman.

On another occasion Gresley chalked on his desk an oval representing a firehole. Towards this he solemnly shovelled imaginary coal with his walking stick, assuring the staff that his new design was good for firemen.

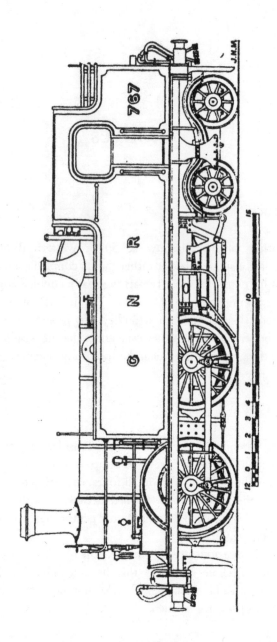

1. Patrick Stirling's Great Northern Railway 0-4-4T with a domeless boiler.

2 - 6 - 0 FREIGHT LOCOMOTIVE Cl. 2F

POWER CLASS: 2F.

Designed by H. G. Ivatt, 1946

200 LBS. PER SQ. INCH.

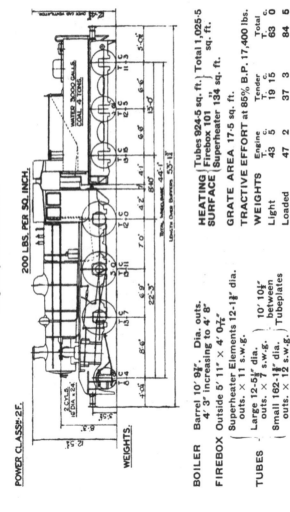

WEIGHTS.

BOILER Barrel 10' 9⅞". Dia. outs.
4' 3" increasing to 4' 8"

FIREBOX Outside 5' 11" × 4' 0⅞"

Superheater Elements 12-1⅜" dia.
outs. × 11 s.w.g.

TUBES Large 12-5⅛" dia.
outs. × 7 s.w.g.
Small 162-1⅞" dia.
outs. × 12 s.w.g.

10' 10½"
between
Tubeplates

HEATING Tubes 924·5 sq. ft. Total 1,025·5
SURFACE Firebox 101 ", sq. ft.
Superheater 134 sq. ft.

GRATE AREA 17·5 sq. ft.

TRACTIVE EFFORT at 85% B.P. 17,400 lbs.

WEIGHTS	Engine		Tender		Total	
	T.	c.	T.	c.	T.	c.
Light	43	5	19	15	63	0
Loaded	47	2	37	3	84	5

2. H. G. Ivatt's LMS class 2F 2-6-0 with 'chamber pot' dome.

9

One day the locomotive superintendent Sir Henry Fowler was found on the floor endeavouring to get through the round back of the office chair. He wanted to find out if he could get through a certain locomotive firehole, which was the same diameter as the back of the chair.

Free Gifts

Although railwaymen were generally honest, sometimes rules were bent. During the coal shortage following the Second World War, one Somerset & Dorset fireman whose garden backed on to the railway had a bright idea.

He would place a large lump of coal on the footplate and then as he approached his home he would *accidentally* kick the coal so that it fell off, bumped down the embankment, went through the wire fence and into his garden.

In reality he made a mistake with the geometry. It went down the embankment, pinged through his neighbour's fence and crashed through the wall of his neighbour's henhouse.

When his neighbour returned home and found a lump of coal with the eggs, he guessed what had happened, went next door and insisted that the driver repair the damage.

When I heard this story, thinking she would be amused, I told it to one of my father's cousins who lived in the same road as the driver. She revealed that it was her father's henhouse – my great uncle!

Another Somerset & Dorset driver, on a train from Highbridge, stole two ducks from a farm. Their owner, suspecting that an engineman was responsible, reported the matter to the police and two detectives awaited the errant driver at Evercreech Junction. They searched the engine high and low but could find no trace of the missing birds and had to go away empty-handed. And where were the ducks? In their natural element of course – swimming in the tender's water tank!

A Long Run

On 20 April 1905 the Great Central Railway operated a 374-mile excursion from Manchester to Plymouth via Swindon with 4-4-2 No. 267. This was the longest record for through-running and was held until the LMS and LNER ran through locomotives from London to Scotland. From Newton Abbot the GCR locomotive was assisted over the steep South Devon banks by a GWR engine. The excursion was repeated on 12 April 1906.

Pulling and Pushing

The Board of Trade required passenger trains to be hauled and never pushed. This ruling could cause the additional expense, at say a station like Templecombe, where a Somerset & Dorset train either had to be pushed into or out of the station depending on its direction because it needed an engine at both ends.

For very short distances this requirement was sometimes overlooked such as SR station at Dorchester which had a Down platform on the main line, but the Up platform on a spur required trains to be backed in.

Some special passenger trains were permitted to be propelled, because working a short-distance branch line train could be very frustrating. This was because an inordinate proportion of time had to be spent at the end of each journey releasing the coupling, brake and heating pipes, the engine running round its train and then having to be re-coupled. Apart from this work involving the footplate crew, the signalman had to pull quite a few levers.

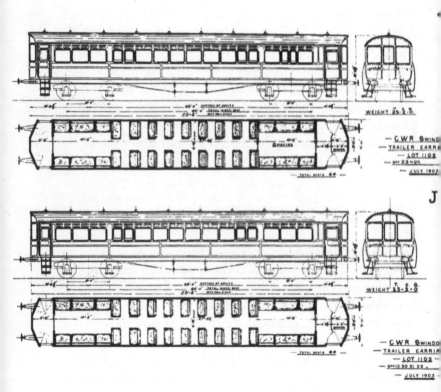

3. A GWR push-pull coach with the driver's control compartment shown on the right.

4. A 0-4-4T propelling an auto-train.

To obviate this nuisance of running round, the auto, or push-pull train was devised. The engine would draw its train to a terminus, and then for the return journey the driver would walk to what had been the rear of the train and drive it from a control vestibule there, the fireman remaining on the locomotive footplate. By mechanical, or air pressure, the driver was able to control, from the other end of the train, the regulator, brakes and whistle on the specially-adapted locomotive. The fireman had to be sufficiently competent to notch up the cut-off at the appropriate time.

Some companies used mechanical rodding between the control compartment and the engine, while others used compressed air. As two coaches was the limit for mechanical operation, if a longer train was required, then the engine was placed in the middle with two coaches on either side. If when a push-pull train was propelling and any goods wagons or vans needed to be added, they had to be placed behind the engine.

An example of how auto-trains secured additional traffic is provided by Plymouth. In 1903 100 trains passed through North Road station during twenty-four hours; in 1907 the number had increased to 250 due to the introduction of auto-trains. The service attracted several railway managers of other companies, one coming from Australia to inspect it.

Some footplate men disliked these auto-trains as it meant that for about half their working time they were solitary. It had its advantages, for apart from saving a lot of work, a driver might very unofficially, if there were no inspectors about, take his girlfriend into the control compartment and have a kiss and a cuddle while the train went from A to B, leaving the entire control of the train to his fireman on the engine.

Time Out of Service

One disadvantage of a steam locomotive is that it is not capable of being used intensively: its firebox and smokebox need frequent cleaning and its boiler washed out, this in addition to other maintenance requirements. A paper read to the Institute of Transport in 1953 by H. H. Phillips, assistant general manager of BR's Western Region, revealed that a locomotive spent only twelve years of its forty years' life expectancy in revenue-earning service – an average engine spent no more than seven hours of every twenty-four in payload movement.

The figures for coaching and freight stock were even more disproportionate: the average coach spent no more than four and a half hours a day earning revenue and a freight wagon no more than fifty-five minutes.

Beyer-Garratt

One type of locomotive which was very popular in Africa, but was rarely used in Britain, was the Beyer-Garratt design. Basically this was a water tank at the front and a tender at the back, both having pistons and driving wheels, while the cab, boiler and

2-6-6-2 "GARRATT" LOCOMOTIVE

Designed by Sir Henry Fowler/Beyer. Peacock, 1927

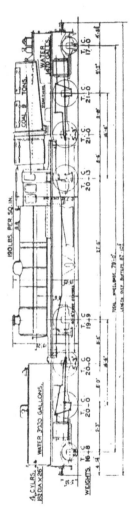

BOILER Barrel 11' 10". Dia. outs.
6' 1⅛" increasing to 6' 3"

FIREBOX Outside 8' 5" × 6' 5¼"

TUBES
Superheater Elements 36-1¼" dia.
outs. × 9 s.w.g.

Large 36-5⅛" dia.
outs. × 7 s.w.g. } 12' 5"
Small 209-2" dia. } between
outs. × 11 s.w.g. } Tubeplates

HEATING SURFACE { Tubes 1,954 sq. ft. } Total 2,137
Firebox 183 " } sq. ft.
Superheater 466 sq. ft.

GRATE AREA 44·5 sq. ft.

TRACTIVE EFFORT at 85% B.P. 45,620 lbs.

WEIGHTS	Front Engine T. c.	Hind Engine T. c.	Total T. c.
Light	58 7	62 0	120 7
Loaded	75 17	79 13	155 10

5. Sir Henry Fowler/Beyer Peacock 2-6-6-2 Garratt.

firebox were slung between the two. It really offered the power of two locomotives, but only needed one crew.

Thirty-three 2-6-0 + 0-6-2 Garratts were used by the LMS on the Toton–Brent and Toton–Wellingborough coal trains and the return empties, their use eliminating much of the double-heading required prior to their introduction. The Garratts were limited to eighty-five wagons in the Up direction only, because the loop at Finedon Road, Wellingborough, could not hold a longer train clear of the running lines.

Garratts were not normally turned – their length precluded them from being turned on anything but a triangle. Their great coal and water capacity gave them a high degree of availability.

One weakness was the length of time taken to replenish the two water tanks as only one could be filled at a time. Firing these large engines could be a formidable task, especially those without rotating coal bunkers which brought the coal forward.

While waiting for his train to be prepared at Washwood Heath, Birmingham, one Garratt fireman filled the box right up to the firehole door and no glow could be seen, only a mass of black coal. This was not normally accepted as good practice, but the Garratt steamed perfectly throughout the whole journey and the fire was not replenished from start to finish at Toton, Long Eaton.

Coal trains worked by Garratts had the habit of becoming divided south of Toton. This was due to the switchback nature of the road which was so undulating that a lengthy train could be on two or three different gradients at once. Great skill in handling was necessary, not only by the driver but also the guard, the secret being to keep the couplings as taut as possible throughout the train to prevent the loose couplings causing snatches. Sometimes as many as six train divisions occurred in one day.

If their builders, Messrs Beyer-Peacock, had been given a free hand, these LMS Garratts would have been excellent machines,

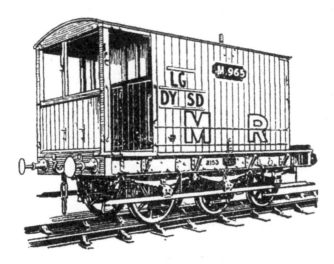

6. A Midland Railway brake van.

but they were instructed to fit Midland class 4F 0-6-0 axle boxes with typical Midland spring gear and Midland short-lap valve gear with poor cylinders and valves. This meant that their maintenance in good condition was virtually unattainable in the 1950s and about 25,000 miles between shop repairs was thought good going, and at that mileage they knocked everywhere and leaked steam at every orifice.

Today narrow gauge Garratts can be enjoyed on the Welsh Highland Railway.

The Most Powerful British Locomotive

On a tractive effort basis, the most powerful steam engine in Britain was the LNER Beyer-Garratt locomotive No. 2395 used for assisting coal trains up the 1 in 40 bank of the Worsborough branch between Wentworth Junction, near Barnsley, and West

Silkstone. The 2-8-0 + 0-8-2 locomotive developed a tractive effort of 72,940 lb.

The next most powerful was the ex-Great Central S1 class 0-8-4T used in hump marshalling yards. With its booster in action it had a tractive effort of 46,900 lb, or 34,525 lb without the booster.

Of the larger classes, the 33 LMS 2-6-0 + 0-6-2 Garratts developed 45,620 lb and the six LNER class P2 2-8-2 used on passenger service between Edinburgh and Aberdeen 43,460 lb.

A Change of Name

Sometimes it was necessary to change the name of an engine. Because it was being repaired at the time it was decided to send No. 6100 *Royal Scot* to the USA, sister engine No. 6151 *The Royal Horse Guardsman* exchanged number and name; similarly for the 1939 visit No. 6229 *Duchess of Hamilton* changed with No. 6220 *Coronation*.

For the funeral of King George VI in 1952, the train carrying his coffin was headed by an engine of the Castle class bearing the name *Windsor Castle*, but it was, in fact, not No. 4082 *Windsor Castle* built in 1924 which had hauled the funeral train of his father King George V in 1936, but No. 7013 *Bristol Castle* built at Swindon in 1948. No. 4082 had been sent to Swindon for overhaul shortly before the death of the king and was thus unavailable. The brass plates on the cab of *Windsor Castle* which commemorated the occasion in 1924 when King George V drove the engine three-quarters of a mile to Swindon station, were also transferred to *Bristol Castle*.

Locomotives Rescue a Ship

On 24 September 1918 disaster overtook the troop ship *Onward* in Folkestone Harbour. Shortly after the servicemen disembarked, smoke was spotted issuing from the ventilators and the alarm was given. Despite rapid action by naval firefighting teams, the blaze quickly spread throughout the ship and to save the harbour installations it became necessary to open the seacocks.

As *Onward* filled with water and settled on the harbour bed, she developed a severe list which increased until she was lying on her port side with the funnels and mast protruding across the harbour.

South Eastern & Chatham Railway 0-4-0ST No. 313 had been used by the port authorities to haul wagons of equipment clear of the blazing vessel and had been left standing just clear of the vessel's bow when the cocks were opened. As *Onward* listed away from the quay, the mooring wires parted and one became entangled around No. 313.

This wire slowly dragged No. 313 towards the harbour and but for the presence of mind of the crew who severed the wire with a cold chisel, she would probably have ended up aboard the scuttled vessel.

In due course salvage operations took place, *Onward* not only having to be floated, but returned to an even keel. To achieve this, compressed air was pumped in while four locomotives on the quay, two 0-6-0s and two 0-6-0Ts, exerted a steady pull and succeeded in dragging her upright.

Working the Glasgow & South Western Railway

In order to prevent a head-on collision on a single line, a train was required to collect a tablet or token of which only one was available. If collected at speed, this could be quite painful and some firemen padded themselves with newspaper. Some enlightened railways had automatic collection where this was done mechanically, while others had some sort of hook.

David L. Smith in *More Glasgow & South Western Nights' Entertainments* tells of Driver Jimmy Sewell having an inexperienced fireman. Jimmy picked up the tablet himself and gave it to his mate with the explicit instruction, 'Look out on your side at the other end of the tunnel. A man'll come out with a thing for catchin' it. Hang the tablet on it.' The fireman, although unskilled, was a willing, conscientious boy. It was a pity that just as they reached the other end of the tunnel an engineer should have set up his theodolite alongside the track!

The 1.00 a.m. goods train from Glasgow to Stranraer could be loaded up to seventy wagons. It was not the hauling that caused a driver problems but the fact that he needed to keep the couplings tight through the dips between Maybole and Girvan. If he reached the bottom of a dip with the couplings hanging slack, then when the line started climbing the weight of the train snatched the loose couplings and could easily break a weak link or drawbar. The golden rule was to go over the summit at Maybole as slowly as possible and gradually increase the engine's speed as the speed of the train increased.

The guards did their bit to help: one using a brake stick to screw the brake handle down tightly, while another had a length of point rodding which he would fix to the brake handle and tramp round like a sailor at a capstan. It was not unknown for the van floors to ignite from the friction between the brake blocks and the wheels.

7. A Glasgow & South Western Railway advertisement.

A Sleepless Night

Years ago on the Glasgow & South Western Railway a heavy goods train had to be taken south from Girvan. Only one engine was available, so the only way of getting a train up the steep Glendoune bank was to take half the train up first, leave those wagons at Pinmore station, return to Girvan for the second half, and then couple up both halves at the summit.

The first half climbed up the bank alright and the engine had just returned to Girvan when Pinmore wired that the first half was 'away' – the wagons were running down the gradient towards Pinwheerry.

Gathering momentum, they dashed through Pinwherry at almost 60 mph. Fortunately the gradient rose very steeply beyond the station and after a mile or so, their momentum was exhausted.

Back they came roaring through Pinwherry and up the gradient towards Pinmore. They continued this see-saw movement until after five or six times they came to rest.

The best bit of the whole affair was the comment the next morning from the permanent way inspector who chanced to stay the night at Pinwherry station house. He was emphatic that he had never tried to sleep at a busier country station; there were, he declared, trains through the night every ten minutes.

Passport Required to Visit Scotland

During the First World War to travel north of Inverness was like visiting a foreign country as a special passport was required to enter the restricted area. It was served by a Naval Express, one in each direction daily, on the 730-mile journey between London and Wick. Almost invariably composed of London & North

SCOTLAND

The

EAST COAST ROUTE

from KING'S CROSS

is the

SHORTEST & QUICKEST

To EDINBURGH - PERTH - DUNDEE
ABERDEEN - INVERNESS - ETC.

EXPRESS SERVICES to GLASGOW,
WEST HIGHLANDS, etc.

Restaurant and Sleeping Car Expresses

WEEK-END TICKETS

SEATS & COMPARTMENTS RESERVED

Booking Fees, 1s., per Seat; 5s., per Compartment.

For all information apply at any L·N·E·R Station or Office. Ask for "ON EITHER SIDE," which pictorially describes features of interest to be seen from the train.

TRAVEL BY

EAST COAST ROUTE

8. An advertisement favouring the East Coast route to Scotland.

Western, Midland and East Coast Joint Stock, and sometimes with carriages from the GWR and other lines, the various liveries presented a cosmopolitan appearance.

Apt Locomotive Names

On 29 May 1955, the first full day of the locomen's strike, a train left Paddington for Cardiff well-loaded and dead on time. And the name of the Castle class engine hauling it? *Defiant*!

In a similar vein, in the 1930s when Eamonn de Valera, prime minister of the Republic of Ireland, was travelling from Liverpool to Euston, the Protestant Edge Hill shedmaster provocatively allocated Royal Scot class No. 6122 *Royal Ulster Rifleman* to haul his train.

Unusual Locomotive Fuel

Although coke was used initially for heating water in a boiler, when the brick arch was invented, this allowed coal to be used and was the common provider of heat in Great Britain, though some countries used wood or peat.

James Holden of the Great Eastern Railway built the first oil-fired British locomotive in 1893, the 2-4-0 *Petrolia*. He used the gas-oil residue which remained following the production of gas for carriage lighting. Steam was initially raised by coal, and then oil took over. Oil flowed on to an open-ended tray designed so that the oil spread evenly over the surface before flowing over the open edge of the tray in the form of a fine film or ribbon. As it fell, it was broken into very minute particles by steam or compressed air.

9. A 1922 advertisement for oil-burning locomotives.

The weight of the oil required was from one-half to two-thirds that of coal, and the savings in labour were effected at engine depots as the oil was supplied by pumps and there were no ashes or clinker to dispose of. Additionally, the boiler tubes did not become clogged, thus giving a locomotive much greater availability.

As coal was cheaper than oil in Britain, the latter was only used during strikes which restricted coal supplies – occurring in 1912, 1921 and 1926. In 1945 when there was a shortage of good steam coal because the best was exported to obtain foreign currency, the GWR equipped some engines for oil firing. Another advantage of oil burners was that the range of an oil-fired engine was approximately half as much again as one using coal.

The Ministry of Transport thought it an excellent scheme and authorised other main-line companies to convert 1,217 engines from coal to oil firing. Then, after many locomotives had been converted and money invested on oil-fuelling plants, the Treasury announced that there was not enough foreign exchange available to purchase the oil!

Pre-Second World War the Southern Railway U class 2-6-0 No. 1629 was fitted experimentally to burn pulverised coal and the necessary plant erected at the Eastbourne locomotive depot. No results were published, but it is believed that they were not sufficiently satisfactory to justify the adoption of the principle.

The experiment was abandoned when one day spontaneous combustion of the pulverised coal in the container occurred, and a black cloud of very finely divided fuel rose into the air due to the force of the explosion and was slowly wafted by the prevailing breeze over the town, upon which it descended with the resemblance of black snow, but with the dissimilarity that it did not melt. The event caused residents much irritation and a lively protest to the railway company by the authorities evoked the assurance that the town had no fear of a recurrence of the incident.

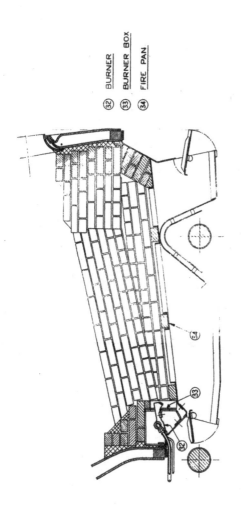

32 BURNER
33 BURNER BOX
34 FIRE PAN

L. M. & S. R.
LOCO DRAWING OFFICE
DE R B Y
D. D. 3845

DIAGRAM IV   ARRANGEMENT OF FIREPAN – OIL BURNING LOCOMOTIVES

10. A 1947 LMS drawing of the firepan arrangement for an oil-burning locomotive.

Sir Ralph Wedgwood's Coal-Saving Appeal

In 1924 Sir Ralph Wedgwood, chief general manager of the LNER, issued a very telling appeal to enginemen on the 7,000 miles of railway under his control. It read:

> Coal costs 22*s* per ton. We use 4¼ million tons a year. Our coal bill is thus £4,675,000. If every locomotive burnt 1 lb of coal less for every mile it ran, the company would use 75,000 tons less in a year and save £80,000. Will every engineman help his running superintendent to get this economy?

Gresley's 'Hush-Hush' Locomotive

In theory, high-pressure steam should be more economical, but in reality the extra complications and increased cost of construction and maintenance offset any saving. Gresley designed a compound 4-6-4 No. 10000 with a boiler pressed to 450 lb containing only half the normal quantity of water, thus saving about five tons and raising steam in about half the time and therefore seeming an excellent proposition. In September 1924 he approached H. Yarrow, who had great experience with water-tube boilers, with a view to a joint project.

The boiler completed in 1929 was quite different from the conventional boiler. The principal section was a top drum almost 28 feet long with an inside diameter of 3 feet. Below the principal section were four smaller drums slung from the top drum by tubes. In place of the normal barrel there was a combustion chamber.

The reason for the engine's failure was the lack of reservoir capacity in the boiler, which made it very difficult to maintain an even pressure for the varying demands of locomotive work, and it caused the problem of obtaining even heating in the long combustion chamber. As the superheater temperature took time to build up after a stop, condensation formed in the low pressure cylinders with an unfortunate subsequent loss of power just when it was needed for acceleration. In 1937 this engine was rebuilt with a conventional 250 lb boiler and externally was similar to the A4 class streamlined Pacifics.

A Peculiar Place for a Chimney

It was decided to construct ten of the BR Standard class 9F 2-10-0s with a Franco-Crosti boiler – an Italian invention designed by Dr Piero Crosti as a means of increasing efficiency.

In an orthodox steam locomotive the firebox gases, after leaving the boiler tubes, are ejected through the chimney carrying away a substantial amount of heat. In the Franco-Crosti system, the normal chimney on the smokebox was closed and gases passed through tubes in a secondary drum before being ejected through a chimney placed on the side of the engine just in front of the firebox.

This secondary drum was preheated to raise the temperature of the feed water so that it entered the boiler at a temperature only slightly less than that of the water already in the boiler. When put to the practical test it was found that the cost of the additional complication offset any fuel saving.

London Transport's Steam Locomotives

Although the London Underground railways were the first in the country to change to electricity, steam was still used for outer-suburban working, the Metropolitan Railway changing from steam to electric haulage at Harrow and later at Rickmansworth.

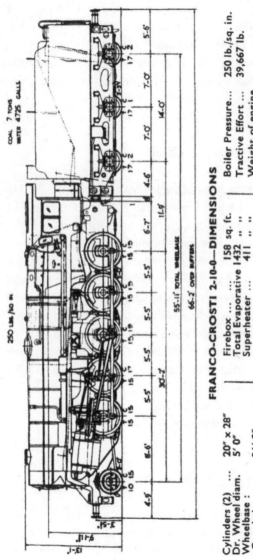

FRANCO-CROSTI 2-10-0—DIMENSIONS

Cylinders (2) ...	20″ × 28″	Firebox	158 sq. ft.	Boiler Pressure...	250 lb./sq. in.
Dr. Wheel diam.	5′ 0″	Total Evaporative	1432 ″ ″	Tractive Effort ...	39,667 lb.
Wheelbase :		Superheater ...	411 ″ ″	Weight of engine	
Coupled	21′ 8″			in working order	90 t. 4 cwt.
Total Engine ...	30′ 2″	Preheater :		Weight of engine	
Engine and Tender	55′ 11″	Tubes	1021 ″ ″	and tender in	
Heating Surface :		Exhaust Steam Jkt.	57 ″ ″	working order ...	141 t. 9 cwt.
Main Boiler :		Grate Area ...	40.2 ″ ″	Tender Type ...	BR1B
Tubes	1274 sq. ft.	Boiler Type ...	BR12		B

11. A BR class 9F 2-10-0 with a Franco-Crosti boiler.

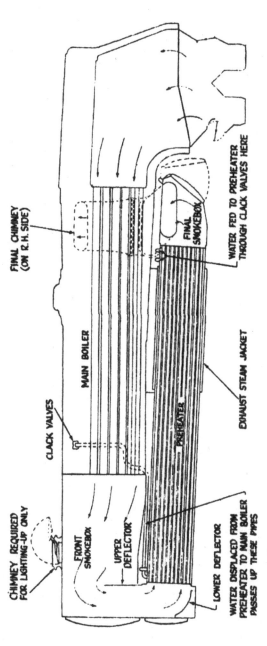

CHIMNEY REQUIRED FOR LIGHTING-UP ONLY

FRONT SMOKEBOX

UPPER DEFLECTOR

LOWER DEFLECTOR

WATER DISPLACED FROM PREHEATER TO MAIN BOILER PASSES UP THESE PIPES

CLACK VALVES

MAIN BOILER

PREHEATER

EXHAUST STEAM JACKET

FINAL CHIMNEY (ON R.H. SIDE)

FINAL SMOKEBOX

WATER FED TO PREHEATER THROUGH CLACK VALVES HERE

12. Arrows indicate the path of combustion air and hot gases through a Franco-Crosti boiler.

In the mid-1930s London Transport transferred its larger engines to the LNER, only retaining smaller ones for working permanent way trains.

No. L34 was a 0-4-2ST built in 1922 whose small dimensions enabled it to pass through tube tunnels. The Central London Railway had two 0-6-0Ts used when the line was under construction and were equipped for burning oil fuel and also condensing. It was curious that London Transport, with its extensive electric network, should have continued to use steam locomotives well after British Railways abandoned them in 1968, London Transport retaining steam until June 1971.

The most curious of all London Transport's lines was the Quainton Road to Brill branch. Originally the Wotton Tramway, it was built to serve the Duke of Buckingham's estate and as no land needed to be purchased, no Parliamentary powers were required. The single track was standard gauge and most of the earthworks were made in the winter when labour was available and cheap, because during that season fewer were required for agricultural work.

When opened in 1871 it was horse-worked, but the following year was operated by Chaplin & Horne using two 6 hp four-wheeled traction engine-like locomotives from Aveling & Porter bought at £400 apiece. Each weighed 10 tons in working order and the single cylinder imparted motion to a flywheel from where a chain connected with the wheels. As these locomotives only travelled at 4–8 mph, the journey of 6½ miles took about 90 minutes. Two Manning Wardle 0-6-0STs replaced the Avelings, though latterly Metropolitan 4-4-0Ts were used which had formerly worked on the Circle line.

The coaches used on the branch were interesting. Based on a GWR broad-gauge design, the four axles were not on bogies, but the necessary flexibility was offered by the axle boxes being able to move laterally in the horn guides.

WOTTON TRAMWAY.

His Grace the Duke of Buckingham and Chandos, Proprietor.

A TRAIN will leave **BRILL STATION** for **QUAINTON** at 6.55 a.m and 2.20 p.m.; and will leave **QUAINTON** for **BRILL** about 9.10 a.m. and 6.5 p.m.

THE RUNNING WILL BE AS UNDER:—

	A.M.	P.M.
Leave Brill	at 6.55	2.20
„ Wood Siding	7.9	2.33
„ Church Siding	7.21	2.46
„ Wotton	7.31	2.55
„ Wescott	7.56	3.25
„ Waddesdon Road	8.20	3.40
Arrive at Quainton	8.33	3.55

	A.M.	P.M.
Leave Quainton	at 9.10	6.5
„ Waddesdon Road	9.33	6.26
„ Wescott	9.45	6.38
„ Wotton	10.10	7.0
„ Church Siding	10.16	7.6
„ Wood Siding	10.38	7.20
Arrive at Brill	10.55	7.40

These times will be adhered to as far as possible, but the running may be delayed, especially on the return journey, by late arrivals of the Trains at Quainton, or from other causes.

R. A. JONES, *Manager.*

Brill, October 1st, 1887.

DE FRAINE, PRINTER, " BUCKS HERALD " OFFICE, AYLESBURY.

13. An early timetable for the Wotton tramway showing an average speed of approximately 4 mph.

33

The Wotton Tramway was important as it had the possibilities of being extended to Oxford, so to this end the Oxford, Aylesbury & Metropolitan Junction Railway was incorporated in 1883. Although still owned by the Oxford & Aylesbury, from 1 December 1899 the line was worked by the Metropolitan Railway. With the formation of the London Transport Passenger Board in 1933, the board took over the line's working, but then made a decision not to run trains beyond Aylesbury, so the branch was closed from 1 December 1935.

Like a New Pin

Most drivers were proud of their engines, keen on them being turned out smartly and giving cleaners tips to burnish the buffers. Some Caledonian drivers removed a portion of paint on the smokebox door to create a polished steel star around the smokebox door handle, or to produce a polished band encircling the smokebox. Some of the Highland Railway Clan class engines had thistles on their smokebox doors.

Artistry

In the 1860s Ted Harrison was a driver on the South Eastern Railway at a time when each driver had his own engine. During quiet periods, Harrison used his artistic talent to decorate the cab. At first he added innocuous items such as stars, but growing bolder, adorned the weather board with scantily clad dancers. These efforts were enjoyed by his colleagues and visiting enginemen.

However, the Strood stationmaster, horrified, immediately sent a report to headquarters at London Bridge and the result was that Harrison was ordered to remove the offending pictures, but complied with extremely bad grace.

Now it was the duty of every stationmaster to make a daily inspection of the toilet facilities and remove any poems, diagrams, or sketches which had appeared on the walls since the previous day.

Harrison, aided and abetted by his colleagues, decided to make this task worthwhile, so one evening painted a large devil chasing a voluptuous blonde across the whitewashed walls.

Next morning the Strood stationmaster, watched by many eyes, made his daily inspection and having absolutely no sense of humour, called for the police. Harrison was proved the culprit and fined two days' pay and ordered to re-whitewash the walls in his own time.

Film Studio Locomotives

Two ex-Great Eastern 0-6-0s were purchased by the cinema studios at Denham for use in films where railway scenes were necessary. In 1939 they were used in Robert Donat's *Goodbye, Mr Chips* and were manned by two ex-King's Cross drivers who drove them up and down the half-mile long studio line according to the director's schedule. Curiously both men had joined the Great Northern Railway at the same time and also passed out at the same time as firemen and as drivers, while only eighteen months separated their respective retirements.

How to Start a Locomotive on a Rising Gradient Without It Slipping

A wise driver takes care when stopping his train on a rising gradient and as far as possible comes to a stop with compressed buffers and slack couplings. This means that the energy stored

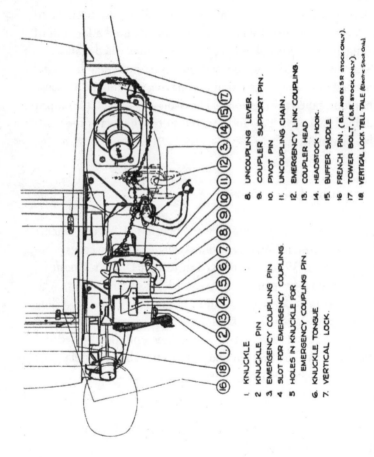

1. KNUCKLE
2. KNUCKLE PIN .
3. EMERGENCY COUPLING PIN
4. SLOT FOR EMERGENCY COUPLING.
5. HOLES IN KNUCKLE FOR
   EMERGENCY COUPLING PIN.
6. KNUCKLE TONGUE
7. VERTICAL LOCK.

8. UNCOUPLING LEVER.
9. COUPLER SUPPORT PIN.
10. PIVOT PIN
11. UNCOUPLING CHAIN.
12. EMERGENCY LINK COUPLING.
13. COUPLER HEAD
14. HEADSTOCK HOOK.
15. BUFFER SADDLE
16. FRENCH PIN . (B.R AND EX S.R STOCK ONLY).
17. TOWER BOLT. (B.R. STOCK ONLY)
18. VERTICAL LOCK TELL TALE (Electric Stock Only)

14. Parts of an automatic buck-eye coupler.

in the compressed buffer springs is added to the tractive force of the engine and so the weight of the train comes on the tender drawbar by degrees, thus the actual start of the engine is made with a relatively light load and so the slipping of the driving wheels is less likely.

This practice was essential with long loose-coupled goods trains at all stops, and this explains the noisiness of a freight train starting from rest as all the couplings one by one are pulled taut. This entails a driver opening his regulator very carefully and then closing it again after the engine had travelled a few feet and was taking the pull of the first wagon; he then repeated this action until the whole train was on the move; then when all the chains were taut he opened the regulator to its fullest extent.

Passenger stock fitted with the buck-eye type of coupler is more difficult to start than stock fitted with link and screw couplings, owing to the spring compression being reduced and there being less 'give' between the vehicles as the strain is taken by the drawbars.

Transformation from London Underground Tank Engine to Tender Engine in Rural Wales

When the Metropolitan District Railway was electrified, its 4-4-0 tank engines became redundant. In 1905 the Cambrian Railways purchased six of these, but found the adhesion weight of 33½ tons on their driving axles, when the side tanks were full, was greater than the Cambrian track and bridges could safely carry. Consequently the engines were restricted to banking and yard-shunting duties.

In order to make them more widely useful, the Cambrian Railways sent one of these engines to Messrs Beyer, Peacock & Co. who, at relatively small cost, removed the side tanks and bunker and converted it into a tender locomotive. In doing this the adhesion weight was reduced to 27½ tons. A large drag casting had to be fitted behind the firebox in order to adjust the centre of gravity after 2 feet 6 inches had been cut from the near end of the frames.

The GWR had a class of engine which was also transformed. Approaching the end of the broad-gauge system, the GWR built several convertible engines, that is, standard gauge engines fitted with broad-gauge axles. One such class of convertible had a 2-4-0T arrangement, but proved so unsteady that the final example was built as a 0-4-4T with short side and back tanks instead of a saddle tank. To a certain extent this modification proved successful and the others of the class were similarly altered, but then between 1899 and 1902 the boilers were turned back to front on their frames and became 4-4-0 tender engines rendering them much more stable.

A Rival Railway at Swindon

Swindon and the GWR were synonymous. Always a rather superior railway, the GWR had its nose put out of joint when on 5 February 1883 the Swindon, Marlborough & Andover Railway opened, thus London & South Western Railway coaches were able to run through from Waterloo to Swindon, providing material evidence of Paddington's competitor right at the heart of the GWR system.

Locomotive Classification

The Big Four used different methods of classifying their locomotive stock. The LNER used a separate letter for each different wheel arrangement, followed by a digit to indicate the particular variety of the type. A second digit could indicate subdivisions due to rebuilding or other alterations. Until 1946 the actual numbering of LNER locomotives was very haphazard.

The LMS engines were classed simply on their power rating with a suffix 'P' or 'F' to indicate whether it was passenger or freight to which the rating referred. Almost all of its locomotives of one class had consecutive numbers.

The GWR adopted the curious plan of making the second digit of the number the class indication, so Hall class 4-6-0s had '9' as the second number, e.g. 4900. If the number of engines in the class exceeded one hundred, the next thousand was used, for example, 5900.

The SR had no systematic practice regarding locomotive numbers, or the distinguishing letters of classes, until Oliver Bulleid introduced a scheme just for engines of his own design. A letter indicated the number of driving axles plus the locomotive's number, for example his first 0-6-0 was C1, while his first 4-6-2 was 21C1, the 21 showing two leading carrying axles and one trailing.

Diesel Railbuses

The LMS opened its luxury Welcombe Hotel at Stratford-upon-Avon on 1 July 1931 and conceived a dramatic new service. Although there was a branch line from Blisworth, on the West Coast line, to Stratford, this would not take guests to the hotel door, so a Karrier Ro-Railer was used, a bus capable of running on either road or rail. Its body, built by Messrs Craven, was like an ordinary contemporary road bus but divided into three sections. The front had accommodation for fourteen passengers facing forward; the rear was a smoking saloon for twelve passengers on longitudinal seats, while between the two saloons was a central vestibule provided with a door on each side. Some of the rear seats tipped to offer additional luggage space. Like the road coaches of the period, provision was made for carrying luggage on the roof. An ingenious device enabled the entrance to be adapted to either ground or platform levels. Heating was by the Thermo-Economic hot-air system.

It was painted in a livery of crimson lake with a white roof. Powered by a six-cylinder 37.4 hp petrol engine, it had a top gear ratio of 7:1 for road use and 4.2:1 for rail, offering a maximum speed of 60 mph and 70 mph respectively, though in reality the Ministry of Transport restricted its speed on the public highway to 30 mph as it did with all heavy vehicles. Petrol consumption on the road was 8 mpg and 16 mpg on rail, showing how much less resistance steel wheels meet when running on steel rails.

Flanged wheels were fitted to the vehicle's axles and on the outside of these were pneumatic-tyred road wheels, each of which was mounted on eccentrics fitted to an axle extension through the rail wheel. When on the road, the road wheels were locked concentrically to the rail wheels, which, being of smaller diameter, were clear of the ground. The rail wheels were the Lang-pattern laminated wheels with detachable steel tyres. This form of wheel possessed resilience and exceptional strength.

For road to rail transfer the Road-Railer was driven to any place where the rail surface was flush with the road, though in practice a special siding at Stratford was used. Then, with the rail wheels directly above the lines, it was driven forward a few yards until it reached a spot where the road surface tapered off. This caused the rail wheels to gradually come into contact with the rails and took the vehicle's weight off the road wheels. The latter, mounted on an eccentric, were raised above rail level by the driver who turned them on their eccentrics and locked them to the chassis by means of a pin. The road wheels did not rotate when the coach was on the rails. The rear wheels were driven by a shaft in the same way as an orthodox road vehicle and were provided with sanding gear. The average time for changeover road to rail or vice versa was approximately four minutes.

Following a series of demonstration runs on the branch between Harpenden and Hemel Hempstead and then on the road beyond, from 23 April 1932 (Shakespeare's birthday) until 2 July 1932 the Road-Railer ran from the hotel, where it was garaged overnight, to the station and then onwards by rail to Blisworth where passengers could change onto a London train. It then returned to Stratford with passengers from London.

Although a mechanical success, at 7 tons 2 cwt it was too heavy for its power and twenty-two seating capacity and was withdrawn after the front axle broke at Byfield in June 1932, the vehicle being withdrawn 2 July 1932.

This experiment did not cause the LMS to give up on bus-based designs and in 1934 they purchased three four-wheeled Leyland Motors 40-seater diesel railbuses which were taken into stock on 30 June 1934.

The body was a bus type, built with sloping ends. There were twenty seats in each of the two saloons, in pairs on either side of a central gangway. From the central doors, the seats faced each end. The driver sat in a small compartment on the left-hand side of each end. Livery was unlined crimson lake with a light coloured band around the waist and skirt.

Its overall length was 41 feet 1 inch and the wheelbase 21 feet. The six-cylinder Leyland engine had an output of 95 hp; drive was via a Lysholm-Smith hydraulic torque converter. In working order a railbus weighed 13 tons 2 cwt. Maximum speed was 56 mph and fuel consumption 13 mpg. Each cost £1,850. Trials took place in February 1934 running over the main line between Preston and Carlisle, while on 21 February 1934 No. 29950 ran from Euston to Watford, the distance of 17½ miles being covered in just over 24 minutes, with 50 mph being maintained for much of the distance. Passengers were impressed by the quality of the ride and the marvellous view forward and the three cars entered regular service in the week ending 14 July 1934. They were allocated to Lower Darwen shed near Blackburn. Early in the Second World War, two of the buses travelled north of the border and shedded at Hamilton.

Due to their lightness they could not be relied on to operate track circuits and so if detained on a running line the guard was required under Rule 55 to proceed to the signal box to remind the signalman of the unit's presence. These railcars were not fitted with standard couplings and buffers, but a special attachment permitted them to be propelled or towed. They were frequently liable to break down. Riding of the cars became poor and subjected passengers in the front seats to violent lateral oscillations. By 1 May 1949 all three were based at Hamilton but only No. 29952 was in use, the others being cannibalised to keep it running. All three were withdrawn in the week ending 28 April 1951.

In 1953 Associated Commercial Vehicles built a train of three railbuses which ran in the Watford area between 1955–9. Initially a private venture, eight more buses were purchased by BR. The fact that they only worked for four years indicates that they were not a roaring success.

In the late 1950s BR was faced with increased costs of working branch trains plus road competition. One idea to either regain traffic, or at least provide more economical working, was to use low-capacity, lightweight, four-wheeled diesel railbuses as a replacement for steam-hauled branch line passenger trains.

In order to be fair to the various British manufacturers, orders were placed with AC Cars; Bristol/Eastern Coach Works; D. Wickham & Co; Park Royal Vehicles and the German, Waggon und Maschinenbau. Each firm supplied five buses with the exception of Bristol/ECW which provided only two. All were

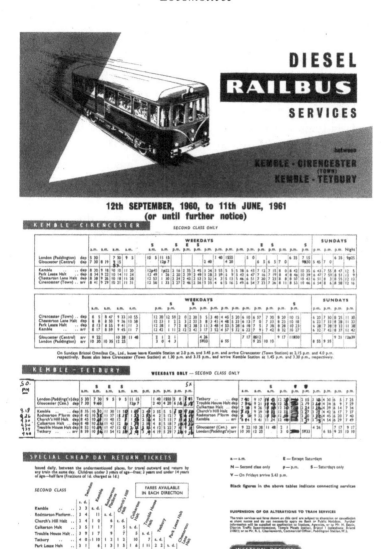

15. Kemble to Cirencester & Tetbury timetable depicting an AC Cars vehicle working the service.

similar in layout, the AC Cars version 36 feet in length, (that is about half the length of a conventional diesel multiple-unit), weighed 11 tons, seated 46 passengers and was fitted with an AEC 150 hp engine. There was a small driving compartment at each end and space for carrying mail and parcels. Retractable steps were fitted for use at rail level halts. The guard issued tickets from a Setright machine much like a contemporary bus conductor.

In the late 1970s a third generation of railbuses appeared. Originally based on a Leyland National bus, the production types looked less bus-like and were named Pacers. Disliked by some, the author enjoys their interesting ride, at times reminiscent of a galloping horse.

The branch line from Stourbridge Junction to Stourbridge Town, a distance of only three quarters of a mile, is the shortest in Britain and appropriately is worked by the shortest vehicle, a Parry People Mover. Designated class 139 it is a gas/flywheel hybrid drive railcar. The basic power is provided by a Ford MVH 420 2.3-litre 64k~W LPG fuel engine, driving through a Newage marine gearbox and 'V' belt drive to a flywheel. Normal braking is by regeneration to the flywheel. The maximum speed of the railcar is 45 mph, though restricted to only 20 mph on the branch. The steepest gradient on the branch is 1 in 67.

A Steam-Diesel Locomotive

The 1920s and 30s brought much new thinking to the railways – steamlining, diesel shunters and diesel railcars. In 1927 a genius came up with the idea of combining a steam and diesel engine.

The Kitson-Still locomotive appeared from the Kitson works in 1927. The 2-6-2T carried a boiler which, in addition to the normal fire tubes, carried tubes and flues carrying heat provided by the diesel cycle of the locomotive. Oil fuel was carried in a tank behind the cab and above a water tank.

The engine had eight cylinders, four at the front and four in front of the cab. The inner end of each cylinder used steam generated by oil-firing to start the locomotive from rest and accelerate it up to about 6 mph. Then the compression ignition system took over, steam was cut off, the oil burner shut down and the heat generated by the diesel engine was used to heat water via the tubes mentioned above. When extra power was needed, such as when climbing a gradient, the oil burner was relit and the inner ends of the cylinders were worked by steam, diesel operation continuing at the other end.

As with many experiments, teething troubles were experienced: excessive vibration of the diesel engine at slow speeds being one, and problems with the oil burner another. When lighting-up there was unequal expansion in the boiler due to the top of the boiler being hot near the fire tubes, but cold at the bottom as there was no heat from the diesel exhaust. This problem was cured by introducing steam from another boiler.

By 1933 all these problems had been ironed out and it regularly worked goods trains over the 43⅗ miles between York and Hull. Curiously the amount of fuel used by the diesel engine was 248 lb and by the burner 247½ lb, though the diesel engine hauled the train for approximately six times the mileage of the steam working. Although the engine finally proved a success, finance was unavailable for it to be built in quantity.

Diesel Railcars

The first really successful diesel railcars were those which first appeared on the GWR in 1933. A 130 bhp AEC diesel engine formed the propulsive unit, the same type as were fitted to

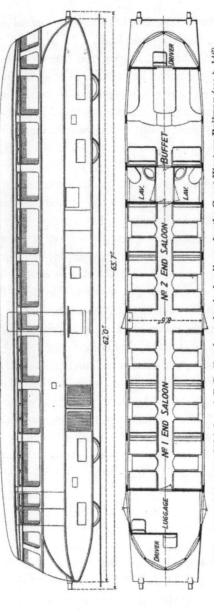

The first of the new 260 b.h.p. A.E.C. diesel-mechanical railcars for the Great Western Railway (*see p.* 146)

16. GWR 260 bhp AEC diesel-mechanical railcar No. 2 built in 1934. It has two-plus-two seating and buffet accommodation.

17. A supplementary ticket issued for travel on the Birmingham to Cardiff streamlined railcar service in 1934.

London buses. The power and transmission components were entirely below the floor. The Park Royal Coachworks body seated sixty-nine passengers in three-plus-two format. Its maximum speed was 60 mph. The body shape was the result of wind-tunnel tests on models at the London Passenger Transport Board's laboratory at Chiswick. Eventually a total of thirty-eight were built and were the basis of the first British Railways diesel railcars.

A Surfeit of Passengers

Although BR welcomed passengers on its new diesel multiple-unit services, in November 1960 a surfeit of them caused a problem.

The 7.13 a.m. Reading to Paddington was stopped five times in four weeks by the weight of passengers depressing the springs to such an extent that the Automatic Train Control apparatus touched the tracks and thus activated the brakes.

A Disaffected Passenger

One generally thinks of the 1930s as the acme of railways in the twentieth century – streamliners running on the LNER and LMS, and the GWR working its *Cheltenham Flyer*. Apparently it was not all perfection as a letter to *The Times* revealed.

Sir, – I have just returned from a visit to Scotland, and I think it is reasonable to give the following account of my journey north.

I left London on one of the midday trains on Friday, December 23. I settled down in the long coach containing thirty-one others in the hopes that so many bodies in such a comparatively small space would create adequate warmth, helped by the company's steam heating. This apparently was too much to hope for, and, after repeated requests for more heat had failed, we resigned ourselves to a cold journey.

At 5 o'clock I went along to try my luck for tea and found an enormous queue waiting patiently in a pitch-dark coach. This coach had a full complement of passengers and had no light from London to Carlisle except for an occasional spell for a few minutes. After standing in this queue for an hour and a half, I eventually won a place in the restaurant car, and, a few minutes after sitting down, the attendant came along and announced that he was very sorry there would be no tea, as they had run out of gas. All the bread and butter, toast, &c., had also run out and we were offered a small tin containing a few chocolate biscuits and some rather dry yellow cake.

I complained bitterly to the attendant, who asked me in reply if I would come along and see the conditions under which they were working. I accepted the invitation, and on reaching the kitchen car I found about four attendants groping about among the shelves, and the only light they had was a dirty old oil lamp.

I arrived at Glasgow nearly two hours late feeling I had had a really good "Raw Deal" and a "Square Meal"! [At this date the Big Four, feeling the serious competition of road transport, sought for a 'Square Deal']

Yours faithfully,

CHARLES C. ALLAN,

Bachelors' Club,

South Audley Street, W. 1

January 7, 1939

One-Off Engines

For economic reasons, railway companies standardised engines, often building many of the same type. Most of the one-off engines were experimental and because of mechanical imperfections, or because the design was unsuited to that railway, no more were built.

One of the most famous was the GWR Pacific *The Great Bear*. She was an engine before her time and owing to her size and weight she was restricted to the London to Bristol run. She was not a favourite of the engineering department as she was liable to derail when taking sharp crossovers and on a few occasions spread the track. For many years *The Great Bear* worked the 6.30 p.m. express from Paddington, returning in the early hours of the morning with a fast goods. In 1923 she was converted into a Castle class 4-6-0 and renamed *Viscount Churchill*.

Another famous one-off was Midland Railway 0-10-0 No. 2290 used for banking up the 1 in 37½ Lickey Incline south of Birmingham. Another ten-coupled engine was the Great Eastern's Decapod No. 20, built in 1903 to demonstrate that steam could give as good acceleration to a suburban train as electricity. Its success defeated an application to Parliament to build a rival electric line serving north-east London. Like *The Great Bear* she was in advance of her time, was too heavy for the road and in due course was converted into a 0-8-0 tender engine.

Sir Cecil Paget, works manager at Derby from 1904 until 1909, designed a 2-6-2 tender engine which would have reduced the amount of double-heading on that line. An outstanding feature was its eight single-acting cylinders with steam distribution by sleeve valves. Another unusual feature was that it had a dry-back firebox with a semi-circular water jacket above. These two innovations for a locomotive were fine on stationary engines, but proved unsuitable due to vibration encountered on a locomotive. Although it reached a speed in excess of 80 mph and certainly had potential, when Paget became superintendent of the Traffic Department he was unable to continue developing his design, others did not share his enthusiasm so it was scrapped in 1915.

A famous solitary engine in Scotland was Caledonian Railway 4-2-2 No. 123, its work on expresses was so excellent that it is surprising that the class was never increased. Fortunately she has been preserved.

In the 1920s the LMS believed that working locomotives at a higher pressure would be more economic and so designed *Fury*, with its boiler mounted on a three-cylinder compound version of a Royal Scot frame. The firebox was partly of water-tube construction and a burst high-pressure tube killed a footplate inspector. Under Stanier, she was rebuilt into the first taper boiler version of the Royal Scots.

In 1926 Beyer Peacock built an experimental Ljungstrom condensing locomotive with turbine propulsion. Fowler agreed that it could be tested on the LMS and it worked express passenger and freight trains. Although its coal consumption was slightly greater than a comparable ordinary engine doing the same work, the condenser saved 84 per cent of water, but this saving was not sufficient to justify its adoption.

4-6-2 PASSENGER LOCOMOTIVE Cl. 7P

"Turbomotive"

Designed by Sir William Stanier, F.R.S., 1935

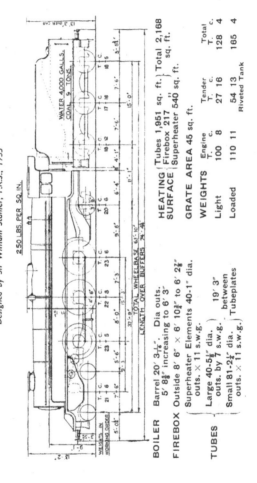

BOILER Barrel 20' 3$\frac{1}{16}$". Dia outs.
5' 8$\frac{1}{2}$" increasing to 6' 3"

FIREBOX Outside 8' 6" × 6' 10$\frac{1}{2}$" to 6' 2$\frac{7}{8}$"
Superheater Elements 40·1" dia.
outs. × 11 s.w.g.

TUBES Large 40-5$\frac{1}{8}$" dia. outs. by 7 s.w.g. } 19' 3" between
Small 81-2$\frac{1}{4}$" dia. outs. × 11 s.w.g. } Tubeplates

HEATING SURFACE Tubes 1,951 sq. ft. Firebox 217 sq. ft. } Total 2,168 sq. ft.
Superheater 540 sq. ft.

GRATE AREA 45 sq. ft.

WEIGHTS	Engine T. c.	Tender T. c.	Total T. c.
Light	100 8	27 16	128 4
Loaded	110 11	54 13	165 4
		Riveted Tank	

18. LMS class 7P 4-6-2 Turbomotive designed by Sir William Stanier in 1935. The turbine is situated above the front bogie.

A few years later Stanier built a Pacific with a turbine drive and popularly known as the 'Turbomotive'. The saving in coal was not sufficient to justify the extra expense of its construction, so it was converted to a reciprocating locomotive and named *Princess Anne*. Unfortunately soon after returning to service it was damaged beyond repair in the Harrow accident of 8 October 1952.

'Leader' – A Revolutionary Locomotive

Oliver Bulleid of the SR had many revolutionary ideas and one of these was the Leader tank engine. It combined the advantages of both a tank and a tender engine by having a large coal and water capacity, being able to run with equal facility in either direction and offering plenty of adhesion with two six-wheel power bogies having 5 feet 1 inch wheels. It was designed to run 80 miles before taking on water and 150 before needing more coal. Maximum speed would be 90 mph and it would be able to run over most of the Southern's tracks.

A driving cab was at each end, while the fireman operated in the central cab. As hitherto driver and fireman had worked together, the fact that they would be solitary did not appeal to some. In practice the central cab became too hot with temperatures of 122 degrees Fahrenheit being recorded.

The Leader made its inaugural run from Brighton Works on 25 June 1949 and when stopping to take on water, it was found that all the water columns were too low to reach the filling point set unusually high, so a small hose coupled to a tap in the porters' office had to be used. During subsequent trials mechanical defects occurred and a further problem was that when the engine was weighed at Eastleigh it was found to be 130½ tons instead of the expected 110 tons, thus severely restricting its availability.

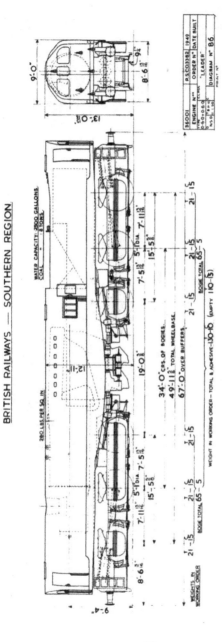

19. Side elevation of Oliver Bulleid's 0-6-0 + 0-6-0 Leader class locomotive.

On 19 November 1949 work on constructing further engines of the class was ordered to stop and R. G. Jarvis of Brighton asked to make a report. He said that the main disadvantages were: its weight restricted the lines over which it could run, while the enclosure and lubrication of the engines axle boxes and springs proved unsatisfactory as were some other of the engine's features. Although Bulleid had retired in September 1949, he requested to be kept in touch with the project, but then asked to be released in March 1950.

Following modifications at Eastleigh, trials commenced on 6 June 1950 but these were not an outstanding success. After further modifications, more trials were held in October of the same year. Unfortunately on one run a workman had failed to secure the smokebox door, so cinders and char fell out and threatened to set the wooden lagging and floor alight while the door itself became warped. Although she reached about 90 mph and a replacement door was readily available from her unfinished sister, the fire was dropped and she never steamed again.

Bulleid and officials from the Irish Railways for which Bulleid was now working, visited Brighton with a view to purchasing No. 36001 and her four unfinished sisters. Presumably they thought better of it as they did not take up the offer.

The money spent on Leader was not entirely wasted because all three of the Southern diesel-electrics used the same body-to-bogie mounting which gave trouble-free service, while the BR Mark 6 bogie had the same damping and cushioning arrangement as was used on the Leader.

Gas Turbine Locomotive

The GWR, always keen on innovation, in 1946 ordered a gas-turbine locomotive from the Swiss firm of Brown-Boveri, only the third such machine in the world. It did not arrive in England until 1950 when it chiefly ran on Paddington–Bristol expresses. It was nicknamed 'Kerosene Castle'.

A second gas-turbine was ordered, this time from Metropolitan-Vickers, and delivered in December 1951. Both locomotives suffered from the defect that they consumed almost as much fuel when idling as when hauling a train, so the system was less efficient than diesel-electric propulsion. With a light load, the Metro-Vickers engine consumed 2.97 gallons per mile, approximately three times the consumption of a diesel-electric.

Methods of Shunting Other than by Locomotive

Horses were used for shunting industrial sidings and also at stations to attach or detach a wagon running as tail traffic to a passenger train, or to move it to a line which had no locomotive access – such as a stub siding with a wagon turntable its only access. The horse was hooked to the side of a pre-loaded van, gave a hearty pull and then stepped out of the way, the impetus fly-shunting the van to buffer up to the train standing at the platform. To ease the work of the horse, it was customary for its keeper to use a pinch bar behind a wheel to help set it in motion. In the event of a horse being unavailable, a man could use a pinch bar to move a wagon.

Railways on the Isle of Wight were individualistic and to avoid specially lighting-up an engine just for a short shunt, a manual geared locomotive was in use at St John's shed, Ryde. *Midget* was a 0-4-0 with extremely small rail wheels and on its decking, and set laterally to the direction of travel, were two large wheels each of which would be turned by a man in mangle-like fashion.

Another method of moving vehicles when a locomotive was unavailable was to use a rope attached to a wagon. The rope was wound round an either electrically powered or hydraulically powered capstan.

Yet a further method was a device, basically a wheel propelled by a petrol engine, fixed between a rail and buffer beam and powerful enough to move a small rake of wagons.

Cable haulage was a method of moving a whole train. The London & Blackwall Railway used this between 1840 and 1849 as did the Glasgow subway 1896 to 1935. In the early days of railways ropes were used to assist trains up steep inclines – the 1 in 70 bank out of Euston was so worked until 1844, while whole trains, including locomotives were hauled up the 1 in 41 out of Glasgow Queen Street station until 1909.

Wind Power on a Railway

Wind caused an accident on the GWR near Wootton Bassett on 20 September 1848. An excursion train collided with a horsebox which the wind had blown on to the main line.

Policeman White, (the forerunner of a signalman), was on duty and had been verbally advised by his colleague Policeman Skull that the horsebox was secure. However, White failed to check that it was correctly scotched with triangular pieces of wood on both sides of the wheels. A public footpath crossed the line by the horsebox and a person could have removed these scotches. The GWR learned from this incident and installed scotch blocks with padlocks at all places where the main line needed protection, and in the 1870s further improved safety by providing trap points which would derail any runaway before it reached the main line.

Spurn Head in Lincolnshire was some miles distant from the nearest habitation. The little community comprising a lifeboat crew, lighthouse staff and employees at a Lloyds' signalling station, were served by a single track railway linking Spurn Head with the village of Kilnsea. It had no connection with any other line.

At one time motive power consisted of an old 0-6-0ST, converted to a 2-4-0ST by the expedient of removing the front part of the coupling rods, which was used to haul the passenger coach, but this locomotive fell out of use. In the 1930s communication was effected by means of a sailing trolley provided for the lifeboat men, and a converted motor car for conveying stores.

Working Trains by Gravity

Some early horse-worked railways were set on a gradient, and such railways as the Stockton & Darlington and the Bristol & Gloucestershire provided a low dandy wagon so that a horse could jump in and have a ride down, thus speeding traffic and increasing the amount of work the animal could perform daily. Until 1939 the Festiniog Railway ran slate trains by gravity from Blaenau Festiniog to Portamadoc, a locomotive hauling them on the return journey.

The West Somerset Mineral Railway was formed to carry iron ore mined on the Brendon Hills down to Watchet where it was ferried across to South Wales. The most outstanding feature of this 13¾-mile-long line was the three-quarter-mile-long Comberow Incline on a gradient of 1 in 4. Gravity, plus a cable, enabled wagons running down the incline to haul empty wagons up. Although a passenger service ran on the flatter portions of the line, for safety reasons no official passenger service ran on the incline, but people were allowed to travel on it for free, albeit at their own risk.

Gravitation was used in hump shunting whereby a train was propelled slowly over a hump, wagons uncoupled, either singly, or in rakes, and run to a nest of sidings, the points being

20. The three-quarter-mile-long Comberow Incline on the West Somerset Mineral Railway.

appropriately altered. This was much more economic than a locomotive going backwards and forwards pushing wagons into a siding and then pulling the rest of the train out.

Gravity could also be used for running round a train at a terminus, a loop line or siding, allowing an engine to move off the main line while the train ran by using gravity.

Illiterate Enginemen Are the Best

The majority of the GWR's earliest engine drivers and firemen were recruited in the north of England by the company's

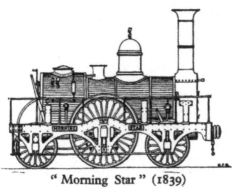

"Morning Star" (1839)

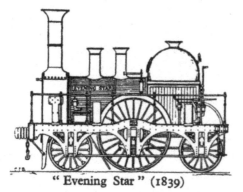

"Evening Star" (1839)

"Red Star" (1840)
As converted to tank engine

21. GWR locomotives driven by illiterate drivers.

locomotive superintendent Daniel Gooch. They were chosen for their mechanical knowledge rather than for their literacy achievements. Brunel, in 1841, claimed that non-reading men were the best drivers as their minds were not so liable to wander. He also stated that 'the best engine driver, now foreman at Reading, can neither read nor write, and so has a clerk'.

James Cudworth's Invention

In the early days of steam locomotives, in order not to produce smoke, engines burnt coke. This was more expensive than coal and James Cudworth, locomotive engineer to the South Eastern Railway, designed a firebox divided longitudinally by a mid-feather which consumed the smoke made when burning coal. The firebox had two firehole doors and the two sides of the box were fired alternately by dropping the coal beneath the doors where most of the gases were given off before the engine's movement caused the incandescent mass to descend towards the front of the steeply sloping grate. Although the idea worked well, the mid-feather was difficult to keep in good repair, yet Cudworth claimed that the South Eastern, between 1865 and 1870, spent less on its fireboxes than any other railway south of the Scottish border.

Although these Cudworth engines were always referred to as coal-burners, in reality they burnt a mixture of two-thirds screened Beamish coal and one-third good quality large coke. When lighting-up, only coke was used. By 1870 the design became obsolete when the deflector plate and brick arch were introduced into conventional and simpler fireboxes allowing coal to be used.

22. The entrance to the Severn Tunnel.

Creating a Stink

When the fireman of a train passing through the Severn Tunnel had an assistant engine in front of him, sometimes this tempted him to take things easy and let the other engine do most of the work.

When the fireman of the leading engine realised that advantage was being taken, it was standard practice to pull the smoke plate out of the firebox on the shovel and urinate on it before replacing it. The obnoxious gas from the evaporated liquid made the engine behind accelerate to get away from the stench. An even better effect could be obtained by throwing rotten fish heads into the firebox.

Locomotive Headcodes

Locomotives carry headlights to give warning of their approach and towards the end of the nineteenth century there was a need to distinguish whether the train carried goods or passengers and whether it was fast or slow. By about 1905 a standard headcode was used by most railways.

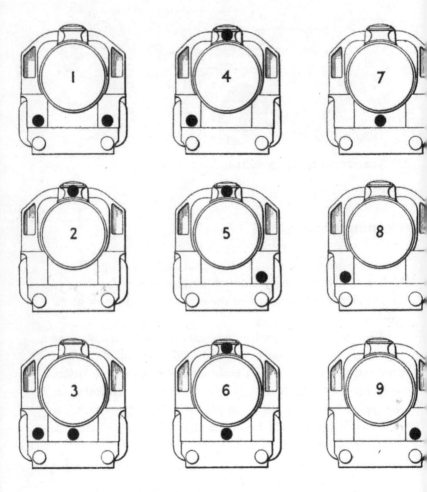

23. Headlight code for classifying trains.

1. Express passenger train, or breakdown train going to clear the line.
2. Ordinary passenger train, or breakdown train returning to the depot.
3. Parcels, newspaper, fish, milk, meat, horse and 'perishable' trains composed of coaching stock.
4. Empty coaching stock, fitted freight, fish or cattle train, not less than one-third of which is fitted with the continuous brake.
5. Express freight or ballast train, of which less than one-third is fitted with the continuous brake.
6. Through freight or ballast train.
7. Light engine or engines coupled together, with one or two brake vans.
8. Through mineral or empty wagon train.
9. Ordinary short distance freight or ballast train, calling at intermediate stations.

The royal train carries four lamps, one on each of the lamp-irons.

The 'Is line clear?' bell signals transmitted between signal boxes vary in accordance with the classification of the train concerned. 'Is line clear for express passenger train?' being four beats in even succession, while 'Is line clear for ordinary passenger train?' being three beats, pause, one beat.

The Great Eastern Railway had a complicated headcode using discs for its London suburban trains. As the discs were white and green, the green discs had a white rim for greater visibility; at night white and green lights were used. The LNER replaced the Great Eastern green disc with blue to avoid the possibility that the green lights of approaching trains could be confused with signals.

The Caledonian Railway and the Glasgow & South Western Railway engines carried an indicator arranged like the two hands of a clock, with movable arms. The 'time' at which the arms were set indicated the route that the train was to follow, perhaps the most familiar being that with the two hands in line at 9.15 which was the main line from Carlisle to Glasgow.

The Southern Railway and its forerunners developed a headcode based on routes rather than class. In 1960 BR introduced a four-character code: the first digit indicating the class, followed by a letter showing the destination, while the last two numbers identified the train.

It is a statutory requirement that every train should carry a tail lamp in order that signalmen have a clear indication that the whole of the train is present and that no part has broken away. Signalmen have to verify that each train is carrying a tail lamp before giving the 'train out of section' call to the signal box at the rear.

24. The tail lamp at the rear of a passenger train.

The Three 9.30 a.m. Trains from Guildford to Waterloo

If you were at Guildford in 1939, at 9.30 a.m., three trains could be seen leaving for the same destination, Waterloo. One travelled by the shortest route via Effingham Junction, 29 miles 74 chains and arrived at 10.23; the 8.20 a.m. from Portsmouth Harbour travelled from Guildford via Woking and reached Waterloo at 10.05 a.m. the distance being 30 miles 27 chains, while the third travelled via Aldershot and Ascot arriving at 11.12 having covered 52 miles 40 chains.

Hard Luck!

The Oxford, Worcester & Wolverhampton Railway was known from its initials as the 'Old Worse & Worse' and at times it certainly earned this nickname.

On 18 October 1855 the 6.45 p.m. express from Oxford to Wolverhampton was rostered to have been hauled from Worcester by No. 24, but as her regulator had failed, the driver was compelled to continue on with No. 14 which had brought the train from Oxford and was really supposed to have finished its day's work at Worcester.

Then at Hartlebury the tyre of No. 14's near trailing wheel jammed against the firebox. Kidderminster was telegraphed for a replacement engine. One was sent, but nearing Hartlebury its driver observed warning lights, reversed and 'lost his regulator'. As there was no other method of shutting off steam, he proceeded to Worcester and reported.

David Joy, the locomotive superintendent started off, arrived at Hartlebury and was about to move the train when the gauge glass broke in the cab and when he attempted to close off steam from the gauge, one of the studs blew out. The result was that another engine had to be sent from Worcester, which eventually took the train onwards and arrived at 3.00 a.m., six hours and eight minutes late, with a total of four engine failures.

Where Could You See Examples of Locomotives from All the Big Four Railways on Passenger Trains in One Station?

The only answer is Oxford – and even that means a little cheating, for although SR and LNER engines could be seen in the GWR station at Oxford, LMS engines did not regularly appear there, but most certainly did in the LMS station adjacent to that of the GWR.

The Manchester Ship Canal Railway

Little known to railway enthusiasts in the south, was the Manchester Ship Canal Railway. The canal, one of the great nineteenth-century civil engineering works, was opened on 21 May 1894 allowing seagoing ships to penetrate into the heart of England, bringing in foodstuffs and raw materials and taking out manufactured products.

The Ship Canal Railway had 33 miles of route and 200 miles of track stretching from Manchester to Ellesmere Port. It owned a fleet of 69 locomotives and over 2,500 wagons. The engines, mostly 0-6-0Ts, were busy shunting traffic among the dockside warehouses.

The line possessed three passenger coaches; one was used for conveying labour supplied by the National Dock Labour Board between the Dock Office Control and Irwell Park Quay, Eccles, another for the resident engineer's permanent staff and the third being the staff inspection saloon.

First World War Relics

In the First World War a standard freight locomotive was required for war service overseas, so 521 Railway Operating Division 2-8-0 engines were built to Robinson's Great Central Railway design for use by the Royal Engineers. In the post-war period when the army no longer required them, no single company wished to purchase them all. Quite a few of the larger companies bought a batch: for example the GWR bought twenty in 1919 that were virtually new and hired a further eighty-four. Most of the loaned engines had been used in France and were in various conditions.

All the borrowed engines were returned to the Government in 1921 and 1922, which dumped them in different locations, until 1924 when they were offered for sale at a much reduced price.

In 1925 the GWR bought eighty at £1,500 each, but after only four months' use, they were withdrawn and sent to the dump at Swindon. It was decided that the best thirty would be 'thoroughly overhauled, fitted with copper fireboxes and painted G. W. standard green', while the other fifty were to be 'touched up and returned to traffic, with steel fireboxes and painted in the original ROD black' and scrapped when no longer fit for traffic. This occurred between 1928 and 1931 to provide a source of spare parts for the remaining engines. It is doubtful if such wholesale scrapping for such a purpose had ever previously taken place. Some of the tenders were used by engines of other GWR classes.

In 1940 a railway enthusiast was surprised to see a tender, in use for water purposes at Stoke Gifford, now the site of Bristol Parkway station. It was still carrying the inscription 'ROD 1983' and the paint would have been applied twenty years previously. It originally belonged to GWR No. 3073 which was the number assumed after the First World War by ROD No. 1983.

This engine had been selected for hauling the staff train of Field-Marshal Sir Douglas Haig and unlike its sister engines special black paint, red-shaded gold figures and the Royal Engineers' crest gave it a very handsome appearance. Haig's train consisted of nine corridor coaches with a heating and power unit coupled next to the engine. The special painting explained why the letters and numbers were still visible over twenty years later.

At the beginning of the Second World War GWR Dean Goods 0-6-0s were sent to the continent with the British Expeditionary Force. It was their second experience of war work as they had also been used in the First World War. More engines were needed so orders were placed with British locomotive firms for the construction of LMS Stanier class 8F 2-8-0s with certain modifications adapting them to French operating conditions. These included Flaman speed recorders, cab-signalling apparatus and Westinghouse air brakes.

Second World War Causes an LMS Engine to Shelter in the USA

At the end of the 1939 World's Fair in New York, the LMS No. 6220 *Coronation* streamlined Pacific locomotive and its Coronation Scot train, which had been exhibited there, were run to Baltimore and partly dismantled in readiness for their return to England. Due to the risk of being sunk by enemy submarines, they were kept in the States for safety. No. 6220 was returned in 1942 and the coaches in 1946.

2-8-0 FREIGHT LOCOMOTIVE Cl. 8F

Designed by Sir William Stanier, F.R.S., 1935

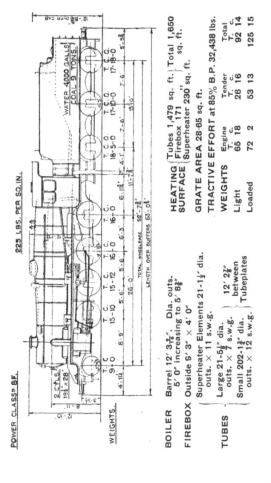

POWER CLASS⁰ 8F.

225 LBS. PER SQ.IN.

WATER 4000 GALLS
COAL 9 TONS.

WEIGHTS

TOTAL WHEELBASE 52-7½
LENGTH OVER BUFFERS 63-0½

BOILER Barrel 12' 3½". Dia. outs.
5' 0" increasing to 5' 8¾"

FIREBOX Outside 9' 3" × 4' 0"

Superheater Elements 21-1¼" dia.
outs. × 11 s.w.g.

TUBES Large 21-5⅛" dia.
outs. × 7 s.w.g. } 12' 2⅞"
Small 202-1¾" dia. } between
outs. × 12 s.w.g. } Tubeplates

HEATING { Tubes 1,479 sq. ft. } Total 1,650
SURFACE { Firebox 171 } sq. ft.
Superheater 230", sq. ft.

GRATE AREA 28-65 sq. ft.

TRACTIVE EFFORT at 85% B.P. 32,438 lbs.

WEIGHTS	Engine T. c.	Tender T. c.	Total T. c.
Light	65 18	26 16	92 14
Loaded	72 2	53 13	125 15

25. Sir William Stanier's class 8F 2-8-0.

Water Troughs

An engine needs to take on water much more frequently than it does coal. Towards the end of the nineteenth century, as the public demanded faster trains, one method of speeding a service was to omit some of the stops required for water. This could be done if an apparatus was devised to allow engines to pick up water at speed.

John Ramsbottom of the London & North Western Railway solved this problem in 1860 by laying troughs between the rails at Mochdre in North Wales. A scoop under the engine's tender was lowered and the speed of the engine forced the water up into the tender. As the troughs obviously had to be laid on a level stretch of track, they could not be placed in just any location. All the principal British railways installed water troughs except the London & South Western Railway, though curiously the large bogie tenders of LSWR 4-6-0s No. 335 and No. 453 to No. 457 were fitted with water scoops. The intention was to lay down

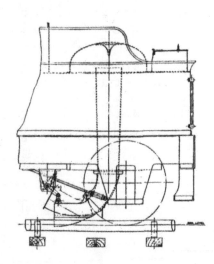

26. The water scoop on a GWR tender for raising water from a trough.

water troughs between Gillingham and Templecombe, but this plan never came to fruition.

A Horse-Drawn Steam Locomotive

The Bristol Port Railway & Pier, running between Bristol and Avonmouth, was originally isolated from the remainder of the British railway system. This meant that locomotives had to be transported on a horse-drawn lorry and on one particularly soft stretch of road no less than sixty animals were required as motive power.

When railway contractors were building a line, it was also sometimes necessary to move locomotives along public roads from the nearest railhead to the site where they were required.

Lost Locomotives

You would not think it possible that an engine could get lost, but this actually happened on the Midland Railway. It was the custom on that line for a driver to always keep his own engine. One day an engine left St Pancras and on arriving at Birmingham, instead of being sent back to London on a train, it was retained and the driver sent home without it.

This locomotive eventually found its way to Gloucester and there it sat, no one knowing to which shed it belonged, hidden in a corner out of the way until it was claimed. In the monthly returns the engine was reported missing and London had to circulate the sheds to find out where the missing engine was.

The Furness Railway also lost an engine, but theirs disappeared down a hole. The area around Lindal Moor was riddled with iron-ore workings and in 1892 a subsidence occurred below the main line. A goods engine was shunting in the vicinity and the track gave way under the weight of the engine. The locomotive fell chimney-first into the chasm which appeared.

It went down slowly at first and the breakdown crew were able to rescue the tender, and, pleased with their success, returned to Barrow to collect heavier equipment needed for the task of raising the engine itself. When they returned they were distressed to see that the engine had entirely disappeared for good.

It seems incredible that in the 1950s a whole train got lost, but this actually happened on the Southern Region.

A fruit train left Ashford at about 12.20 a.m. and should have arrived at Maidstone an hour and a half later. It failed to do so. Orpington control office informed the headquarters of the Kent police at Maidstone and a patrol car was sent to pick up the stationmaster and find the train. It was eventually found at Hollingbourne, two stops down the line from Maidstone: the engine had broken down.

On the same region, a visiting Western Region engine caused a fracas among railway officials. She was No. 5956 *Horsley Hall* which had left Paddington with a crowd of holidaymakers and travelled via Clapham Junction and Redhill because a bridge was down at Guildford. At Redhill came trouble. A keen-eyed official there remarked: 'That engine should not be on this line. She's a restricted type.' (Some structures on Southern routes were slightly too narrow for Western engines). So into Redhill shed went *Horsley Hall* and the argument began.

Western Region: Please may we have our engine back?
Southern Region: With pleasure – but the rules say it can't go along our line.
Western Region: How are we going to get it back?
Southern Region: You'll have to take it to pieces and carry it back by lorry.

Fortunately a compromise was reached and the Southern let it travel over their line back to the Western Region as long as it did not exceed 15 mph.

Running on the Spot

The London & North Western Railway had some compound engines with four cylinders. The two high pressure ones drove one pair of driving wheels and two low pressure cylinders drove the other. To make the engine ride better, Francis Webb, the designer, believed it best not to couple the two sets of driving wheels. This led to curious things happening. It was not unknown when starting off with a heavy train for the wheels to slip, the valve gear to get out of order and for each pair of driving wheels to turn in opposite directions.

In the 1950s two engines were at the head of a fairly light train. The guard waved his flag, the drivers opened their regulators, but amazingly the train would not move. After struggling for some minutes trying to get the train into motion, it was discovered that one engine was in reverse.

On another occasion an engine slipped when starting. The driver tried to close the regulator, but to his dismay found it was jammed open. The wheels spun round and round and when he eventually managed to shut it, the wheels had worn deep grooves in the rails which had to be replaced.

Getting Back Together

In the nineteenth century an express was travelling along when suddenly the coupling pin between the engine and tender broke. The locomotive shot ahead, breaking the side links and pulling the feed water bags out. Fortunately neither of the crew was on the fall plate between the engine and tender. The driver was standing on the engine by his regulator, while the fireman was back on the tender, shovelling the last of the coal forward, for they were near the end of their journey and the coal near the front had been burnt.

The fireman instinctively moved towards the tender brake handle to stop the train, but the enterprising driver ordered him to let the train run on and get the spare coupling pin from the back of the tool box.

While the fireman did this and lifted the fall plate, the driver slowed down so that his engine was now buffered up to the tender. He reversed the engine against the momentum of the train, so that the drawbar spring would be extended and they succeeded in dropping in the coupling pin.

They had only ten more miles to run before reaching their destination and the boiler had sufficient water for the remainder of the journey.

When they stopped at their destination they connected the feed water bags and as there had been no delay to the train, thought it was not worth the trouble of writing out a complicated report.

Unfortunately for them, some farm labourers at work near the line saw the engine shoot away from the tender and gossiped about this strange sight in the neighbouring town. The stationmaster heard about it and investigated. Senior officials praised the footplate crew for their ingenuity, but advised them that it would have been a wiser decision to stop.

A Near Collision

In the nineteenth century a Down express was at the head of a gradient on a single line and the driver knew that as he had a long, heavy train, he would have to brake earlier than usual. This was before the days of the automatic brake working on the wheels of all the coaches, so the only brakes available were on the engine and in the guard's van.

The fireman applied the tender brake just to rub the wheels, but the train still gained speed. The fireman screwed it on harder and harder, but it had no effect. The driver himself tried to turn it on more, but realised it was fully applied.

He gave some short, sharp whistles which were the signal for the guard to put on his brake, but all to no avail, for the train still gained speed.

The driver was now very worried. He knew that 5 miles further on was a passing station where he was timed to cross the Up Mail. The only thing he could do was to keep sounding his whistle as a warning.

The stationmaster at the crossing station heard the whistle echoing among the hills and fortunately guessed what was happening. He knew the Mail had left the previous station and that he must do something to prevent a head-on collision.

He leapt on the back of a horse which belonged to a gentleman doing business at the station and galloped through the goods yard and along the line.

The track here was level and the stationmaster hoped that the driver of the runaway express would be able to get it under control on this section.

The Mail appeared in the distance and the stationmaster signalled the driver to stop, it grinding past him with the brakes full on.

Meanwhile the driver of the runaway express had managed to get his train under control on the level stretch and stopped it before it struck the Mail.

And the cause of the express running away? FISH. Yes, fish. A goods train had been up the bank before the express came down and oil from the fish had run through the cracks in the floors of the vans, down the axle guards and on to the rails. The Down express had picked up the oil on its wheels and this prevented the brakes from working efficiently.

Crows Stop a Train

In about 1900 some crows stopped a GWR goods train.

At that period the axle boxes on goods wagons were filled with yellow grease which crows regarded as a great delicacy. Quite a number of empty goods wagons for the West of England had accumulated in the sidings at Didcot and an engine and brake van were sent to take them on to Swindon.

This train of empties steamed out of Didcot, but at Challow were stopped by the signalman who reported that he had seen sparks coming from several hot axle boxes.

The train was carefully examined and it was found that on several wagons the axle box covers were loose and easily lifted, while others were open and lifted right up. The railwaymen did not need to be good detectives to discover who had sabotaged the train. Crows were responsible and had eaten the yellow grease and left the marks of their feet behind.

27. A Didcot luggage label.

Second World War

During the Second World War there were many curiosities to be seen on the railways, one of the most interesting being the class 160 USA-built 2-8-0s. Rather similar in size and shape to the British 2-8-0 Austerity engines based on Stanier's LMS class 8F 2-8-0s, they had a definite transatlantic appearance. An unusual feature to British eyes was the long-combined sandbox and dome on top of the boiler. The running plate was high, at the time it looked odd, but in post-war days it did not seem as strange as British locomotive designers adopted that feature to allow easy accessibility.

The USA engines were well-equipped with braking power. They had a steam brake on the engine and Westinghouse and vacuum brakes for the train. The large tender was carried on two four-wheeled bogies – this at a time when most British tenders were six-wheeled.

Following D-Day, the author saw trains of five or six dead USA engines passing Bath en route from the docks to Swindon before being sent to the continent. Sometimes they were hauled by a live class 160, but more usually by a GWR 2-8-0. Spotters had a fruitful time as many new numbers could be collected in a very short time, but one had to be pretty smart to get them all down before they passed out of view.

Some 0-6-0Ts also came from the USA and these were very ugly. The author only saw one and that was being hauled between Bath and Bristol minus its motion. In the post-war period the SR purchased some for use at Southampton Docks.

Following D-Day ambulance trains could be seen made up of converted coaches and luggage vans, and were generally hauled by LNER class B12/3 4-6-0s, these engines having the useful capability of being able to travel over almost any line due to their relatively light weight.

Before the Second World War the author had seen SR engines working a few trains between Portsmouth and Bristol; but now saw LNER engines heading ambulance trains at Bath. To complete the Big Four he was lucky enough to see an LMS 0-6-0 on the GWR, it having been lent to replace the GWR Dean Goods 0-6-0s commandeered by the War Department.

The government had ordered the GWR to construct Stanier class 8F 2-8-0s and these appeared in LMS livery and numbers. They were seen frequently on the GWR at Bath and on one occasion the author saw two double-heading a goods train. Curiously, in British Railways' use they actually outlived GWR locomotives built at Swindon, No. 48476 being one of the engines used on the Railway & Correspondence Society's last steam-hauled special on 4 August 1968.

Towards the end of hostilities the author saw prisoner-of-war trains, and guards could be seen standing in the corridors. Signalmen had orders not to stop these trains, as this would have made escape easier.

Main Line Passes Through the Middle of a Locomotive Works

For some time after the establishment of a railway works at Wolverton for the building and repair of locomotives, the main line of the London & Birmingham Railway passed through the actual works area and between some of the shops.

In due course it was found inconvenient to have passenger and goods trains passing through the works area, so the main line was deviated to pass on the east side of the works. The former main line was retained, but used for the conveyance of material and the movements of new and repaired rolling stock.

A South Eastern Railway Engine Is Impounded by Customs

In October 1886 SER 0-6-0T No. 152 was impounded by Her Majesty's Customs at Folkestone. This was because her crew had smuggled eleven bottles of brandy in her coal bunker. She spent more than a month in a siding on the harbour quay with her wheels and motion sealed and the footplate boarded up. It was eventually returned to the SER after its crew had been fined and dismissed from the company's service.

2

Workforce

Calne in the Second World War

During the Second World War, to ease booking at small stations, which could experience a surge of traffic at weekends, special arrangements were made. For example, on Thursday evenings a member of the Calne station booking office staff travelled on a railway lorry to Compton Bassett RAF station and another to a similar establishment at Yatesbury. To travel on these vehicles the clerks had to hold a special pass. On arrival at the camps they sold tickets thus avoiding long queues forming at the station at weekends. This procedure allowed servicemen holding a pre-booked ticket to step straight on to a train. Each travelling booking clerk had a small case labelled 'Camp A' or 'Camp B' containing tickets for the main destinations, blanks being made out for other places. The total collected from the two camps could sometimes amount to over £1,000 and it was said that on these occasions it was left overnight at Calne police station for safekeeping.

The Air Ministry endeavoured to route personnel by rail as much as possible and minimise the distance travelled by road, but sometimes this policy was carried to excess. On one occasion a party from Compton Bassett to Lyneham travelled by coach from Compton Bassett to Calne; by rail from Calne to Dauntsey;

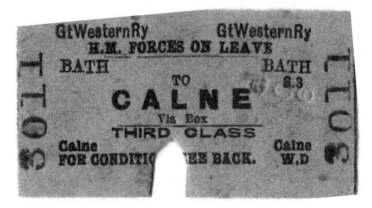

28. An HM Forces on Leave ticket from Bath to Calne.

and then by coach from Dauntsey to Lyneham. This involved a rail journey of 11¾ miles plus 7 miles by road, against a direct road distance of 4 miles!

Curiosities at Swindon Works

The GWR's Swindon Works had quite a few curiosities. All the workshops had sparrows living in them and as they had been there for about 130 years, they became modified. Compared with a standard sparrow, the Swindon variety had two flight feathers missing on each wing and yellow feathers around its throat. They were fed by the men and never went out, so during the holidays workmen went in to feed both them and the cats. Rabbits were also found within the works, some having rust in their intestines due to the rusty land on which they grazed.

The very loud works hooter was one of the special features of the factory. Men walked in from a distance of 9 miles or more and in the nineteenth century when personal and domestic

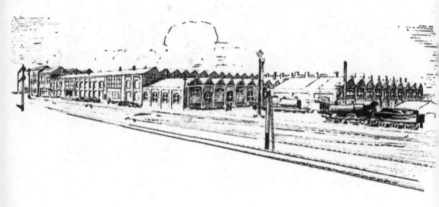

29. The GWR locomotive works at Swindon.

30. The entrance to the GWR locomotive works at Swindon.

31. The GWR Mechanics' Institute at Swindon.

timepieces were beyond the pocket of many, such a warning was necessary. Initially a large bell was used, but by 1867 a hooter had come into use, loud enough to be heard at Highworth and Cricklade 6 miles away. It was blown for ten minutes at 5.20 a.m., for three minutes at 5.50 a.m. and one minute at 6.00 a.m.

In 1872 Lord Bolingbroke complained that it woke him prematurely from his seat at Lydiard Park 3½ miles to the north-west of the works. The Local Government Board at first came down on the side of the GWR, but then revoked the sanction of the hooter and it was only through the ingenuity of the Hon. F. W. Cadogan, at that time MP for the Cricklade Division, which included Swindon, that a solution was found.

Another hooter was fixed on the roof within a few yards of the disputed one and, as Cadogan pointed out, although the original hooter might not be blown, no injunction had been granted against the second one, which, incidentally, was louder than the first. The beauty of this process was that it could be repeated indefinitely, a fact apparently recognised by the authorities for the matter was allowed to drop. A writer in 1935 said that the hooter had been heard on at least one occasion at Bourton-on-the-Water, 25 miles distant. In the 1960s when it was no longer a requirement for workers to be woken, people complained and the hooters were lowered by 30 feet. The final hooters were ships' sirens.

One curiosity of Swindon Works was a tall chimney made from old locomotive boilers bolted together.

The Mechanics' Institute was a great and important feature of the town. It provided facilities for mutual improvement classes as well as a theatre and a library; as no municipal library being provided in Swindon until 1943, schoolchildren proceeded in a crocodile to the GWR Library once a week. This GWR library closed in 1961. To keep abreast of social changes, in 1959 the institute became the BR Staff Association.

SWINDON WORKS HOOTER					
	MONDAY to THURSDAY			FRIDAY	
	TIME	DURATION		TIME	DURATION
M O R N I N G	6·45	17 SECS		6·45	17 SECS
	7·20	12 SECS		7·20	12 SECS
	7·25	7 SECS		7·25	7 SECS
	7·30	12 SECS		7·30	12 SECS
	12·30	12 SECS		1·30	12 SECS
A F T E R N O O N	1:05	12 SECS			
	1·10	7 SECS			
	1·15	12 SECS			
	4·30	12 SECS			

32. The GWR Swindon Works hooter timetable 24 August 1982.

SWINDON

MECHANICS' INSTITUTION.

SYALLABUS OF A COURSE OF SIX

LECTURES

TO BE DELIVERED IN THE

SCHOOL ROOM, NEW SWINDON,

On ALTERNATE MONDAYS, at Seven o'Clock in the Evening.

LECTURE 1st, December 8th,

By Dr. RYAN,

Of the Royal Polytechnic Institution, London,

On HEAT.—Its Sources—Effects and Phenomena—Latent and Sensible Heat—Vaporization and Boutigny's Experiments.

LECTURE 2nd, December 22nd,

By Dr. RYAN, on PNEUMATIC CHEMISTRY.—The Chemical Composition of Air—The Pressure and Elasticity of the Atmosphere—Combustion—Respiration—Ventilation.

LECTURE 3rd, January 5th,

The subject of this Lecture will be announced at the previous Lecture.

LECTURE 4th, January 19th,

BY EDWD. COWPER, ESQ.,

Lecturer on the Mechanical Arts, at King's College, London,

On PAPER MAKING.—Papyrus—Paper from Linen Rag—Cutting the Rag—Grinding into Pulp—Bleaching—Making by hand—the Mould, &c.—Making by Machinery—Pulp Strainer—Fourdrinier's Machine—Dickinson's Machine—Sizing—Cutting—Silk thread in postage Envelopes.

LECTURE 5th, February 2nd,

By EDWARD COWPER, Esq., on PRINTING AND PRINTING MACHINERY.—The first printed Books—The common Printing Press—Stanhope Press—First idea of Printing with Machinery—Nicholson Steam Printing Machines—Koenig—Donkin—Applegath and Cowper—Napier—Rich—Book Machines The Times Newspaper Machine.

LECTURE 6th, February 16th,

The subject of this Lecture will be announced in the previous Lectures.

The Swindon Great Western Band will be in attendance to play some favourite Airs before and after the Lectures.

Tickets of Admission to be had of Mr. ANN, of Swindon; Mr. BRAID, the Secretary of the Institution; and from any Member of the Council.—Price of Admission, Reserved Seats for the Course of Lectures, 5s.—For a single Lecture 1s.—Persons employed in the Works, not Members of the Institution for a single Lecture 6d., who may take with them a Lady on the payment of 3d.—Members of the Institution admitted Free, and with the privilege of taking in one Lady Free.

DORE, PRINTER, SWINDON.

33. GWR Mechanics' Institute handbill for lectures in 1847/8.

In 1845 the GWR opened a school, initially for children of its employees, but later admitting others. Fees were four pence weekly for juniors and two pence for infants, children of non-GWR children having to pay a shilling. In 1874 the GWR built a larger school and in 1881 handed its 1,600 pupils to the care of the local authority school board.

The GWR Medical Fund provided doctors' surgeries and a dispensary. By 1948 the GWR Medical Fund Society Hospital could deal with the population of 40,000; in fact the National Health Service was based largely on the GWR scheme. The GWR even had its own hearse, so truly looked after its employees from the cradle to the grave. The GWR also provided a park, swimming pool and Turkish baths. GWR employees at Swindon had their own savings bank which gave slightly higher interest than the main banks.

The GWR supplied coal and timber to its employees at advantageous prices. Coal was delivered, but timber had to be collected from the GWR Wood Wharf. Two grades were supplied: refuse (bark etc) and old timber, the latter being more expensive. The entrance to the wood wharf was at ground level and timber tipped down a chute from rail level about 20 feet above. In order to collect the purchase ticket, the attendant lowered a tin can on a piece of string or chain, the purchaser placed the ticket in the tin and it was drawn up to check whether it was for 'old timber' or 'refuse'. In hard times, often 'refuse' was ordered but with a penny or two dropped in the tin together with the 'refuse' ticket; this often resulted in good quality 'old timber' being supplied.

One of the features of Swindon Works was the annual trip during the first week of July. This week was chosen because it was earlier than holidays given by most factories elsewhere, in order that locomotives taking those on the Swindon trip would not be taken from paying passengers at the height of the season a few weeks later. The majority of locomotives used on the trip trains

(No. 584.)

R U L E S

OF THE

Great Western, Bristol and Exeter,

AND

South Wales Railways

PROVIDENT SOCIETY,

ESTABLISHED AT

PADDINGTON TERMINUS, MIDDLESEX,

DECEMBER 22ND, 1838.

Altered and Revised 15th June, 1852.

LONDON:

PRINTED BY MORTIMER AND DARBY, 141, STRAND.

MDCCCLV.

34. Title page of *Rules of the Great Western, Bristol and Exeter, and South Wales Railways Provident Society*, 1855.

were stock engines – that is locomotives recently released from the works; coaches came from the carriage store at Newburn.

The trip started in 1849 when 500 workmen travelled to Oxford by special train. It developed through the years and in 1908 no less than 24,565 workers and their families were carried away from Swindon in the early morning by twenty-two special trains before most of the ordinary traffic started. Weymouth, or 'Swindon-by-the-Sea', was the most popular destination favoured by 6,171; other specials ran to London, Weston-super-Mare, Winchester, South Wales and the west and north of England. Two trains ran to Southsea via the Midland & South Western Junction Railway, these consisting of London & South Western Railway stock hauled by a T9 class 4-4-0 which always ran tender-first with empty stock, even though it could have been turned at Swindon. To ease congestion, trip trains did not use the passenger station but left from various parts of the works, portable steps giving access from ground level.

In 1913 the trip was extended to a whole week and in 1939 27,000 left Swindon in thirty special trains. On Wednesdays, shops normally closed for the rest of the day at lunchtime, but during trip week they closed for the whole of Wednesday, practically everyone going off and leaving Swindon like a ghost town. On Friday evening trip trains arrived back at Swindon.

Trip week was really a lock-out for workmen until a week's paid holiday was given in 1938, extended to a fortnight ten years later. With the increase in car ownership, numbers using the trip trains dwindled until they ceased in 1960, ordinary trains being able to cope with the numbers who wished to travel by rail. In 1976 British Railways said that it 'arranged one or two special trains because there were enough employees going to the same place to justify it'.

To celebrate Queen Victoria's Jubilee in 1887 the GWR decided to mark the event with a fete and tea in the park. To provide the expected 15,000 people with a cup of tea, some method better than boiling kettles on a stove was needed. The problem was given to the locomotive department which came up with the plan of boiling water in locomotive tenders.

The original idea involved emptying tea chests into tenders filled with cold water and then turning live steam from an engine into the mixture. The drawback was that, should someone have turned the wrong handle and started the injectors working, the cones of the latter would have become blocked with tea leaves and the fete temporarily stopped while another engine was fetched.

The modified idea was utilising the old tenders normally used as water tanks which trundled between Kemble Junction and Swindon. The tanks needed cleaning out and were in such a poor state that the man who climbed inside to do the job came out in about ten seconds with the remark that if tea was to be made in those tanks he would turn over a new leaf and drink beer for the rest of his life. He made a good job of cleaning them and the resulting beverage only had a moderate tang.

Taps were fixed in the sides of the tenders and they were placed in the siding nearest the park. A goods engine was connected to them by steam pipe, steam was blown into the tenders one by one and the merrymakers filled their tea urns from the taps. It is understood that despite the tang, the doctors had no more stomach problems than usual to deal with during the following week. The whole scheme was a veritable locomotive triumph for the cause of temperance – the man who cleaned the tenders alone excepted.

British Drivers in France

After the First World War some of the British Army's Railway Operating Division drivers were invited to remain in France and drive for the Paris, Lyon & Marseilles Railway. On one occasion a Midland & Great Northern Railway driver was found in charge of a GWR 53XX class 2-6-0 between Paris and Marseilles.

Tips

In 1858 the general manager of the South Eastern Railway issued a circular saying that any servant of the company seen to demand or receive a tip from a passenger would be instantly dismissed.

One evening H. W. Williams, agent at Reading, was on the platform just prior to the departure of a train when he spotted Guard Barrett receiving sixpence from a lady in a carriage. On turning round, the guard immediately saw that the stationmaster had also observed the donation. Thinking quickly, he rushed to the bookstall, bought a newspaper and took it to the lady together with her change.

Williams remarked to the guard: 'That was a narrow shave for you,' to which he received the reply, 'Well, sir, I don't care what trouble I get into, so long as I get out of it!'

Right and Left on the Footplate

The custom of driving along the left-hand side of the road became established in Great Britain in the distant past, but was not made legal until relatively recent times. It was usual for the driver of a horse-drawn vehicle to sit on, or towards the right-hand side to enable him to judge the distance between his and an oncoming vehicle, or to ascertain whether one in front could be overtaken, more easily.

Likewise, with the coming of the railway locomotive the right-hand side was given to the driver so that he could check

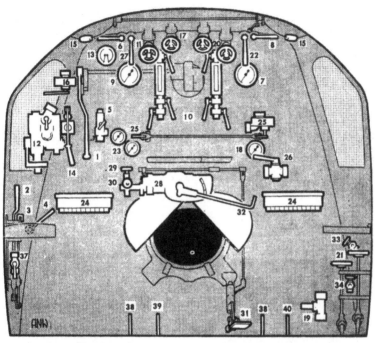

"West Country" cab.
1 Regulator handle
2 Cylinder cock lever
3 Steam reverser setting indicator
4 Steam reverser control lever
5 Steam reverser lubricator
6 Steam reverser steam valve
7 Boiler pressure gauge
8 ditto isolating valve
9 Steam Chest pressure gauge
10 Water level gauges
11 Ejector steam valve
12 Ejector & vacuum brake control
13 Duplex vacuum gauge
14 Engine steam brake
15 Whistle
16 Blower
17 Train heating
18 ditto pressure gauge
19 ditto relief valve
20 Two steam valves for injectors
21 Injector steam & water controls
22 Steam to cylinder lubricating atomiser
23 Lubricating oil pressure gauges
24 Axlebox oilers
25 Steam sanding
26 Steam to electric generator
27 Steam for firehole door cylinder,
28 Firedoor cylinder
29 Firedoor cylinder inlet valve
30 Firedoor cylinder drain cock
31 Firedoor cylinder operating pedal
32 Firedoor hand lever
33 Water valve for hose
34 Tender spray valve
37 Windscreen water spray
38 Two rocking grate controls
39 Drop grate
40 Ash hopper doors

35. An SR 4-6-2 West Country class cab layout showing the regulator handle towards the left.

if anything was amiss with the adjacent track and observe any signals made to him by a train coming in the opposite direction.

Gradually the opposite practice made a footing. Some lines such as the London & North Western, Lancashire & Yorkshire and some Scottish railways transferred the driver to the left so that at most stations the driver could more easily see the guard giving the 'Right Away'. Some locomotive engineers, such as the Drummonds, took their own practice with them when going to another company and there was at least one example of the driver's position being changed over by one engineer and reversed by his successor.

At the 1923 Grouping, the new enlarged railway companies found themselves with locomotives having both kinds of drive. The LMS, LNER and SR decided to make the left-hand drive standard, while the GWR continued to use the right-hand position and convert any engines with left-hand drive that came into its possession, such as those of the Midland & South Western Junction Railway.

Similarly with signals: the logical course was to place them on the left-hand side of the line, but on railways with right-hand drive many were situated on the 'wrong' side to give better sighting at a distance.

In his report on the 4 November 1940 accident at Norton Fitzwarren (see page 180) Sir Alan Mount, Chief Inspector of Railways observed that with right-hand drive and signals for adjacent lines located correctly to the left of each, a driver on the left-hand line of two looks more readily and directly at the signal which does not apply to him, than the one he should pay heed to and this could contribute to a momentary mistake.

Sir Herbert Walker's Management

Roger Arnold as a young lad first encountered Sir Herbert Walker, general manager of the London & South Western Railway, in 1912 just before the *Titanic* sailed. His parents and brothers and sisters had been invited to lunch with Captain Smith and afterwards were shown over the ship.

On their return home from Southampton they had to change at Fareham for the Meon Valley line. Arnold recorded:

> We approached Fareham and just as our train came to a halt, I espied another M7 0-4-4 tank heading a two-coach salmon and umber outfit standing in the bay. The guard was fingering his green flag ready to wave it just as we drew to a halt. But he did not!
>
> A stentorian roar from the footbridge came like a thunderclap to Guard Grant. 'George Grant, hold that train!'

Roger Arnold saw a huge, square-shouldered man in a tweed overcoat, with pince-nez gold spectacles, coming down and hurtling over the timber crossing from the island to the bay platform with the alacrity of a young athlete rather than a staid man in his forties. With his furled umbrella like a foil at the ready he came up to the startled guard. 'Your name is George Grant? Mine is Herbert Ashcombe Walker. You were about to start this train before the passengers from the 5.50 p.m. from Southampton could join, although this is the last train up the Meon Valley today!'

By this time the capless stationmaster came running up to see what had caused the disturbance. Before he could collect his thoughts, Walker was speaking again. 'Your name is Peter Cooper; does this heinous thing take place every evening? If it does, let me assure you it will not happen again without your coming to Waterloo.' A faint cheer arose from passengers within earshot.

By then Walker had boarded the train and from a first class compartment was asking Cooper if he could telephone Alton. 'Yes, sir.' 'Then tell Mr Smith that this train connects with the 8.20 p.m. to Surbiton and Waterloo and if it does not do so then *he* can come to Waterloo and see me in the morning!'

Locomotive Livery

As far as possible, railway companies wished to have an attractive locomotive at the head of a train and many liveries were most handsome. However, when the Midland Railway took over the London, Tilbury & Southend Railway in 1912, a shortage of motive power in the first year made it necessary to place engines in service as soon as possible after repairs. This meant that some locomotives were returned from the shops to work either unpainted, or in their grey priming coats, or in their original green livery with the name painted out (the Midland did not approve of locomotives being named), and large Midland numerals substituted.

Why Did the SR Use Malachite Green?

Three senior SR officials were discussing the merits of various shades and colours for rolling stock and failed to come to a unified agreement.

The general manager, Sir Herbert Walker, went to an optician's shop where reels of spectacle cord were displayed in the window. He dashed in, emerged quickly with a length of green cord, produced a pair of nail scissors and cut off a piece for each of the officers. He retained the rest of the reel. He pronounced:

'Argument shall cease; that will be the colour Southern engines and coaches shall be painted in future. This reel shall remain in my office safe as a standard to which reference shall be made.' When Oliver Bulleid became responsible for the livery of SR locomotives and coaches, the choice of malachite green was thus made by a general manager who had retired a fortnight before Bulleid's appointment began.

Red for Danger

London & South Western Railway staff were instructed to wear red neckties so that they would always have an emergency danger signal to hand.

How the Shunter's Pole Was Invented

For most of the nineteenth century being a shunter was a most dangerous and unpleasant job because the operation of coupling and uncoupling meant creeping under the buffers and handling heavy iron chains. Whatever the weather, snow or ice, rain or wind, the shunter had to actually manhandle the couplings. While doing so, sometimes the engine drew the wagons too far apart and the coupling would not reach, or pushed the wagons against the shunter. There were no yard lamps, the shunter's hand-lamp being the only illumination and he could not take this with him between the wagons because he needed both hands for the task of coupling, or uncoupling. On a wet day there was the added danger that when wearing a mackintosh and going between the buffers, in stooping to handle the chains between moving wagons, his mackintosh could be caught by a wheel and pull him to death.

In the early days there were no brakes on goods wagons and men had to use hand scotches and sprags. Like most of the other railway servants, shunters worked from 6 a.m. to 6 p.m. They were not supplied with leggings and were only given an overcoat once every two years. No separate cabin was available for the use by shunters, so the goods office was the men's only refuge against rain, or in which to dry wet clothes or eat their meals.

The old, dangerous way of creeping under wagon buffers and handling chains when coupling or uncoupling was accepted as inevitable, until an imaginative goods guard used a length of gas pipe to avoid having to stoop to uncouple – he had invented the shunting pole.

In order to induce men to use a shunting pole, railway companies offered prizes to those most efficient at using them. So well did this succeed that a dextrous shunter could couple and uncouple twenty trucks in exactly two minutes. This safer and more convenient method of coupling by using a pole soon spread countrywide.

Guards Who Have Lost Their Trains

Everyone admired the deft way in which a guard swung himself into his van as a train glided out of a station, but such a polished performance was not always seen. One Scottish guard early in the British Railways era waved off his train and then lost it. Enveloped by blinding sleet and by steam from beneath the coaches, he was unable to see the guard's van as the train accelerated past him. He jumped down on to the line and gave chase. At the next station a mile distant he arrived breathless to find his train waiting.

Another guard lost his train through being kind and helpful. One day, in the dark, a lady and child boarded the train at Farrington Gurney Halt on the Bristol to Frome line. In helping

36. A third class Radstock West to Midsomer Norton & Welton ticket.

her into the van with her pram, the guard accidentally knocked his hand-lamp to the green aspect. The train smartly accelerated away to Midsomer Norton, leaving him on the platform. He went to the nearby public house and phoned Midsomer Norton for a taxi to collect him.

An SR guard had a different experience. An electric train from Maidstone to London should have stopped at Bromley South, but went straight through. The motorman, realising his mistake, brought it to a stop beyond the platform. The guard, following British Railways' procedure, got out and walked back to seek permission for the train to go back into the station. After he had taken a few steps, he heard the train move off on its non-stop run to Victoria. However, it was stopped at the next station for him to catch up.

Ambulance Train

In the 1880s life at Hawes Junction on the Settle & Carlisle line was lonely. If someone fell ill during the night and a doctor was required, two platelayers were called. They placed a trolley on the line and using gravity, rode on it down the 6 miles from Hawes Junction to Hawes to summon a doctor.

Normally the doctor arrived at Hawes Junction by road, but in the event of a very serious illness, the North Eastern Railway engine was taken out of the shed and sent down to Hawes to collect him and he also returned by the same unofficial method.

When the permanent way-trolley was used, it was returned the next day to the junction behind the afternoon freight, the platelayers taking it in turn to hold on to the brake van's drawbar – a seemingly risky practice.

Porter's Tip

One porter at Wellington, Somerset, went all out to seek good tips and had an eye for spotting rich old ladies needing help into a first class compartment. He opened the door, carried in the luggage and held out his hand. Other porters at this station, believing his actions unfair, sought to teach him a lesson.

One day the platform inspector and a guard devised a plan. When this over-greedy porter helped someone into a compartment, the guard quickly blew his whistle before the porter could get out.

As the train left, his colleagues saw him gesticulating, so they called out: 'It's all right, we'll have the train stopped at Whiteball.'

They were true to their word and at Whiteball signal box the train stopped allowing the porter to scrounge a lift on a returning bank engine, the driver of which was aware of the lesson being taught and anxious to be part of it.

He opened the regulator wide and the engine sped through Whiteball Tunnel at about 70 mph, the darkness and the rocking scaring the porter … but that was not all! The driver feigned a heart attack and collapsed on the floor.

The highly terrified porter said to the fireman: 'Can't you stop it?' The fireman, also in on the trick, replied: 'No, don't know how, I only came on the job last week!'

Hearing this, the porter climbed down the cab steps ready to jump off – but was then informed it was a joke. He learned his lesson and never went all out to seek large tips again.

Porters' Kindness

In 1958 a woman passenger at Euston sought out the stationmaster just before her train left for North Wales to complain that a porter, to whom she had entrusted with a pound note so that he could get change for his tip, had disappeared.

The other porters, hearing of this deceit, made a collection among themselves to reimburse her and asked that a letter be sent regretting that such a thing should happen at their station.

Taken Unawares

In 1953 station porter Bernard Betts made a trip from Leeds to London in his shirt sleeves.

He was placing luggage in the Up 4.35 p.m. *Queen of Scots* express for a passenger who had arrived only just in the nick of time, and he himself did not have time to get out before the train started.

He threw two notes from the train: one to the Leeds Central stationmaster explaining why he was not on duty and a second explaining to his mother why he had gone to London. He returned on the 10.47 p.m. from King's Cross which got him home at 3.30 a.m. the next morning.

R. I. P.

An aged chief mechanical engineer had wearied his fellow club members for a long time with his chatter of locomotive boilers and cylinders, so his decease was greeted with a certain amount of relief.

'How exactly did he come by his end?' asked one club member of another.

'The old bore had a stroke I believe,' was the reply, 'result of high pressure y'know.'

Haunted Station

A town-bred railwayman stationed at a lonely spot on the West Highland Railway where it crossed Rannoch Moor, wrote to his employers:

> Sir,
> With reference to my application of the 15th inst., I would respectfully point out to you that my grounds for applying for a transfer are that I am unable to stay any longer here as the house that I am in shows visible signs of it being haunted.
>
> The extraordinary moving of furniture at night and other signs leaves no room for doubt. I am unable to sleep at night with the strain. This has occurred for some time now, and I appeal to you to investigate the matter. My workmate and bedmate confirm my statement.

This appeal was successful in securing his transfer to less psychic surroundings.

Timber!

The following letter appeared in the *Daily Telegraph* in November 2000:

> Sir,
> A colleague tells me his local stationmaster made the following announcement yesterday:
>   'We are sorry for the substantial delay. This is due to leaves on the lines, and further due to those leaves still being attached to the trees.'

Force of Habit

In 1935 a witness at Wood Green Court stated regarding the defendant: 'He used to be a railway guard and has a nasty habit of slamming doors.'

Dangerous Hat

Ladies' hats can interfere with efficient railway working. At Sittingbourne, Kent, in the autumn of 1911, a woman wearing a hat with a large green plume was saying goodbye to her friends when suddenly the train started. The engine driver, seeing the green plume bobbing about, took it to be the guard's green flag.

A New Method of Learning the Road

The LNER was very much a go-ahead company and was not slow in adopting modern methods. In 1934, to aid footplate men learning the road, it exhibited silent films depicting the line ahead over particularly busy sections of the line where signals were numerous and complicated. The films were taken from the front of a saloon propelled at 20 mph.

Aspirates

A GWR railway officer was travelling down the line and when his train stopped at Ealing Broadway he heard the station name announced as 'H-Ealing, H-Ealing Broadway'.

This was too much for the officer who put his head out of the window and beckoned the caller saying 'What is your name, my man?' He replied, 'Johnson, sir.'

At Hanwell the officer was again aroused upon hearing the name of that station given as ''Anwell, 'Anwell and Elthorne'.

Again the officer asked for the caller's name. 'Thomson,' the man replied, at the same time adding that he hoped he had done nothing wrong. 'Oh no,' said the official, 'you are quite all right, my man. But there is just one thing; I shall see that you change places with Johnson of Ealing.'

GWR – a Great Way Round

A passenger panted up just as a long distance express was moving out of Paddington. He managed to board the train and thrust his head through the window. 'All right for Westbourne Park?' he called to a porter on the platform. 'Yes sir,' was the reply, 'change at Torquay!'

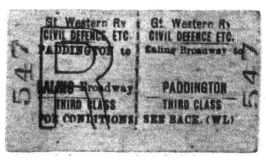

37. A Second World War civil defence worker's return ticket from Paddington to Ealing Broadway.

38. An Ealing Broadway luggage label.

Odd Names

The London Midland Region employees' magazine *Carry On* in 1949 carried the following piece:

Strange Names on the L.M.R.

Mr Ham, Mr Butter and Mr Stew; this strange mixture of names is to be found among the 1,121 stationmasters on the L.M.R. There is also a Cook, Baker and Kitchin. For seasoning there are two Mr Salts and a Mr Pepper.

Two Gardeners, but only one Plant and one Leaf are included. There are two Mr Bishops, one of them at Dean Lane and the other at Castleford, and a Mr Dance at Fidler's Ferry. Colour is provided by Stationmasters Gray, Green, Brown, Black and four Whites.

The rural flavour is provided by Messrs Hill, Dale, Lea, Park, Field, Lane and Meadows, one Church and two Bells, two Swifts, a Wren and a Finch, a Farmer, a Sheppard, two Lambs and a Ram.

Perhaps the strangest coincidence in names is that of Stationmaster Porter of Stonebridge Park.

Farewell

A note of pathos was struck in a passenger guard's journal of 28 September 1935. Working the 10.35 a.m. Cardiff to Portsmouth, Guard A. King of Portsmouth entered: 'This is the last journal to be submitted to you by me; so good-bye. All signals off.'

The *Southern Railway Magazine* in which this piece appeared commented: 'It is hoped that Mr King, who celebrated the occasion by arriving at Portsmouth six minutes before the booked time, will continue to have a clear run of health and happiness.'

Firing the Baby

One day when a mother was ill, the father, a locomotive fireman, had the task of feeding their infant son, aged two, using a spoon.

Hearing the child spluttering and apparently choking, the agitated mother rushed in to see what was happening.

The father explained that he always: 'Led off with one under the fire door; then one left; one right and one well down the far end.' The 'far end' in this case corresponded with the unfortunate child's throat.

The Drawing Office

That a chain is only as strong as its weakest link was proved when a junior draughtsman disturbed the serenity of an otherwise smooth-running organisation.

In preparing a plan to depict a derelict siding which was to be lifted, he inadvertently applied the indicating colour to an adjacent colliery siding in daily use.

When the time came for lifting the redundant track, those responsible for executing the instructions on the plan, considered that it was 'their's not to reason why; but their's but to do or die', and lifted the wrong siding. It was left to a higher power to explain the following day its disappearance to a somewhat puzzled colliery management.

On another occasion the same genius was instructed to prepare a plan for a derailment. Possibly because his duties also included drawings of sites where renewals, or new works, were envisaged, the fruits of his labours were found on completion to be headed: 'Site of Proposed Accident'.

Locomotive Driving by Contract

It is not generally known that at one time it was the custom on a number of railways in England for engine drivers to enter into formal agreements with the companies to work trains at a certain sum per mile.

The custom arose in the very earliest days of railways, as in 1830 the drivers of the Stockton & Darlington Railway were paid a farthing per ton-mile, out of which they had to find coal and oil and pay themselves and their firemen. The company was responsible for maintaining the engines in good repair.

On some parts of the Eastern Counties Railway trains were worked by contract and it is on record that one driver stationed at Peterborough had his price for working goods trains advanced in December 1854 from 5¼*d* per mile to 5½*d*. A few years later, a driver working the passenger traffic between London, Enfield and Hertford was paid 3 $^{7}/_{8}d$ per train-mile.

The driver had to sign an agreement in the presence of a witness; he had to pay his fireman and cleaner; provide firewood for lighting-up, coal or coke for running, oil, tallow and suchlike necessities. He had also, out of the same money, to repair and pay for the cost of certain repairs, giving all necessary assistance himself on shed days. However he did not have to provide articles of iron, brass, copper or steel, or pay for labour when the engine went into shops for general repairs or repairs due to accidents beyond his control.

For an assisting engine he had to pay 3*d* per mile, but if he was required to pilot or assist another engine he received 2*d* for every mile out and home. The drivers purchased their fuel and stores from the company.

Essays on the Backs of LNER Handbills

Taking their cue from nature, which abhors a vacuum, in the late 1920s the LNER publicity department hit on the idea of utilising the backs of handbills for disseminating information dealing with various phases of the company's activities. For instance, on the back of a bill relating to a football match to be held at Northumberland Park on 22 February 1930 was a short, readable article dealing with the distinct personalities of the great London termini; while on a second and third handbill in the same connection were articles, equally readable, on *Weekend Wisdom* and *Footplate Favourites* respectively.

Railway Tickets

Thomas Edmondson, a Quaker, apprenticed as a cabinet-maker, eventually began his own furniture business, but it failed. He joined the Newcastle & Carlisle Railway and was appointed stationmaster of Milton. Dissatisfied with the booking system derived from stagecoach days whereby every ticket had to be written by hand, torn from a book and a counterfoil filled in, Edmondson felt that there must be a simpler way. In 1838 he devised a much better system using pre-printed tickets measuring $1^3/_{16}$ of an inch by 2¼ inches and having a thickness of $^1/_{32}$ of an inch, serially numbered. This was done by four wheels which automatically rotated by a pusher as the former rose and fell. Each wheel had the ten digits cut on the edge and every time the unit wheel moved round once, a stud on it came into contact with a projection on the tens wheel and advanced it one figure. The tens wheel similarly moved the hundreds wheel and the hundreds, the thousands so that 10,000 tickets from 0 to 9999 inclusive could be printed from one setting of the machine.

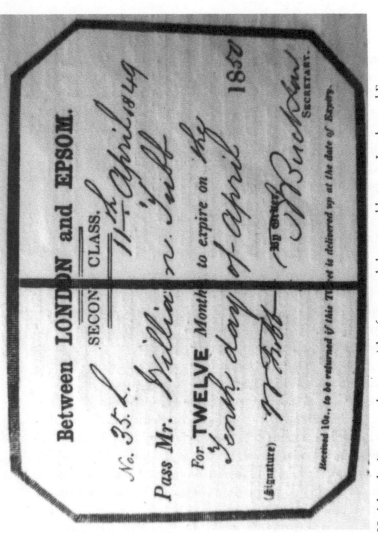

39. A handwritten annual season ticket for second class travel between London and Epsom.

40. A reusable Leicester & Swannington metal railway ticket of 1832.

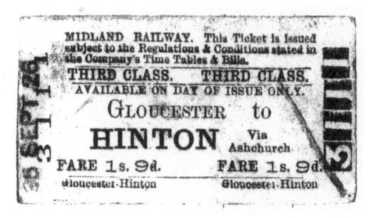

41. An Edmondson ticket printed by the Midland Railway: the serial number shows 3111 and the date stamp on the left 25 September 1926 (this would have been in the LMS era).

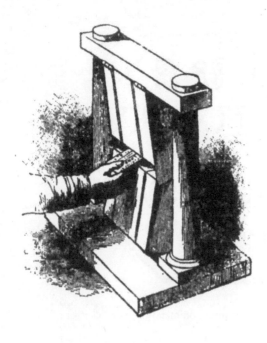

42. An Edmondson
date stamp press.

He invented the date stamp whereby the action of inserting a ticket into a press caused the date to be printed on the ticket by an inked ribbon. Using his woodworking skills, the first dating presses were of wood, but later, with John Blaylock, a Carlisle clockmaker and iron-founder, they were produced in metal.

Initially tickets were taken as needed from the top of the packets which rested on springs which pressed them upwards. Later it was found more convenient to sell the lowest ticket first.

Edmondson's invention became known to Captain Laws of the Manchester & Leeds Railway and he was offered a post at Oldham Road at double his old salary and while there shared his expertise. In 1841 he left to establish his ticket business trading under the name of his son, John B. Edmondson.

Charges for use of his system were on a mileage basis. For a railway 30 miles in length the cost was £15 annually plus £5 for every additional 5 miles of line.

All railways adopted Edmondson's system, the GWR adopting it in April 1845 paying him £75 per annum on the first 300 miles of line plus 5s annually for each subsequent mile.

George Bradshaw

George Bradshaw was born at Salford on 29 July 1801 and after leaving school was apprenticed to an engraver. In 1820 he moved to Belfast and set up his own engraving business. When it proved unsuccessful, he moved to Manchester and in 1827 began to specialise in map engraving. He added letter press printing to his activities and William T. Blacklock became a partner. Bradshaw's first railway timetable was a purely local publication and his first general timetable appeared in October 1839. It was dated '10th Mo. 19th, 1839' – a peculiarity which Bradshaw favoured in view of the fact that being a Quaker, he objected to the adoption of heathen deities in the names of the months.

Measuring 4½ inches by 3 inches, timetable No. 1 only contained details of northern railways, No. 2 only the southern railways, while No. 3 was a compilation of both volumes. Curiously, although *Bradshaw's Railway Time Tables* appeared on the title page, the cover bore the words *Bradshaw's Railway Companion*. One of Bradshaw's quirks was that the cover bore an inch measure.

Bradshaw's Railway Guide, 6 inches by 4¾ inches with a yellow wrapper, as compared to the hard case *Companion*, first became a regularly monthly publication in December 1841.

A curiosity in the numbering was that the March 1845 of the *Guide* was No. 40, but the April 1845 edition jumped in error to No. 141, successive issues continuing from this number. Canon Reginald B. Fellows in the *Railway Magazine*, June 1935 edition,

BRADSHAW'S

𝕽𝖆𝖎𝖑𝖜𝖆𝖞 𝕿𝖎𝖒𝖊 𝕿𝖆𝖇𝖑𝖊𝖘,

AND ASSISTANT TO

RAILWAY TRAVELLING,

WITH

ILLUSTRATIVE MAPS & PLANS.

AUTHOR OF

BRADSHAW'S MAP AND SECTION OF THE
RAILWAYS OF GREAT BRITAIN,
5FT. 4IN. BY 3FT. 4IN.

PRICE IN SHEETS . . . 1 11 6
MOUNTED 2 10 0

AND SOLD BY G. BRADSHAW, BROWN-STREET,
MANCHESTER;
AND WYLD, CHARING CROSS, LONDON.

PRICE ONE SHILLING.

LONDON:

SHEPHERD AND SUTTON, AND WYLD,
CHARING CROSS.

AND SOLD BY ALL BOOKSELLERS AND
RAILWAY COMPANIES.

10th Mo. 25th, 1839.   **(No. 3)**

43. Title page of *Bradshaw's Railway Time Tables* of 25 October 1839
– the first to show timetables of the whole country.

PRIVATE.—Not for distribution to the Public.

JANUARY, 1918, and until further notice.

OFFICIALLY EVERY MONTH

Under the Patronage of HIS MAJESTY THE KING.
The Royal Family, both Houses of Parliament, all the Government Offices,
Banks, and other Public Offices, &c., &c.

BRADSHAW'S

GENERAL RAILWAY AND STEAM NAVIGATION

GUIDE

FOR GREAT BRITAIN AND IRELAND,

PUBLISHERS' PROOF.

LONDON & NORTH WESTERN RAILWAY SECTION.
For Service use only.

L. & N. W. Railway.
Euston, Station, N.W.I.

I. T. WILLIAMS,
Acting General Manager.

[Copyright reserved, see next page.

44. Cover of a Bradshaw reprint used by the London & North Western Railway during the latter part of the First World War.

believes this was not a mistake but was made deliberately in order to make the *Guide* appear longer established than was actually the case, with the object of facilitating a canvass for advertisements at a time when Bradshaw was being subjected to severe competition. The same ruse was made in Bradshaw's *Threepenny Guide for all the Railways of England, Wales, and Scotland* a volume half the price of his other *Guide*.

In June 1847 Bradshaw produced his first *Continental Railway Guide*. In 1853 he visited Christiana, now Oslo, at a time when cholera was raging. Unfortunately he succumbed and died there on 8 September.

In 1917 railway companies were dropping the issue of their own timetables and in April 1917 the GWR arranged for the relevant section of *Bradshaw* to be reprinted for use by its staff. Other railway companies followed suit.

The last *Guide* was for May 1961, and subsequently BR did not provide a one-volume replacement as it continued to issue individual timetables for each of the six regions until 1974, when a single volume was produced covering the whole of BR.

Forty Years in the Same Signal Box

W. H. Seward who became a signalman in 1898, worked in the same signal box at Burlescombe, Devon, for over forty years. This could well have been a record.

Free Coal

An East Anglian character living in the Fens, made use of the Aunt Sally-mindedness of locomotive crews. In his garden he erected an enormous gaily-painted tin cat. Temptation was too much. Crews of passing trains could never resist throwing a lump of coal at the cat. The result was that he never needed to buy any fuel.

A Free Pheasant

Beside the Swindon to Highworth branch was Stanton Great Wood, a pheasant covert where it was not unknown for a lump of coal to be aimed at a bird from a passing locomotive. On one such occasion the crew was unable to retrieve their prey on that journey, but stopped on the next. Just as the fireman was about to pick up his poachings, it was jerked away by the gamekeeper who had watched the whole episode. When questioned by the railway authorities, the footplate men denied that coal had been misappropriated, but this was hard to accept when no less than five sackfuls were recovered from the lineside.

One driver 'learning the road' on this branch before taking over driving duties the following week, intelligently placed an inverted tin on a fence post as a marker where he should apply the brakes before stopping at a level crossing which, as an economy measure, was not manned but required to be opened by the fireman.

Unfortunately when actually driving, he missed seeing the tin and went through the crossing, the remains of the gates hanging on his buffer beam. To compound the situation, leaves strewn across the track added to his problems as they caused the wheels to skid and so stopping was less rapid than it might have been.

Another Free Pheasant

Years ago a goods train was slowly struggling up an incline in the west of England when the fireman spotted a pheasant not far from the line. Love of adventure dominating honesty, he hurled a lump of coal at the bird, killing it. He climbed down from the slowly moving engine and collected his poachings.

Remorse coming to him after he had stored it away in the engine's locker, he offered it to his driver who rightly refused the gift. It seemed a pity to waste the bird so it was disposed of in the best possible manner – he gave it to his vicar!

How the Problem of Frozen Toilets Was Overcome

In the severe winter of 1963 the toilets at one Southern Region station became frozen. Staff wishing to 'spend a penny' had to catch a train to the next station to fulfil their needs.

It Came Off in Me 'And!

A gatekeeper at one of the level crossings on the Malmesbury branch failed to open the gate in time and the train 'dashed through, shivering them to atoms'. It appeared that the old man in charge of the crossing could not get out of his house in time, owing to the door handle coming off in his hand.

Free Produce

Branch lines, especially the 'goods only' kind, gave locomotive crews more scope for obtaining freebies than busy main lines where keeping to a schedule was most important.

Near the terminus of the Thornbury branch in Gloucestershire, delicious watercress grew beside the track and it was not unknown for the daily goods train to stop and the engine crew to jump off the footplate and pick some.

Just outside one of the tunnels on the branch snails could be found on a wall. One driver collected them, placed them on the back of the firebox and when cooked, prised their flesh out with a safety pin.

On the same branch in the 1950s one driver was anxious to have some mistletoe for his Christmas decorations. Unable to find any, he thought the wisest thing to do would be to consult the local policeman. This he did and the constable informed him of a convenient orchard near the railway and told him that he would be quite safe from the farmer's prying eyes because an embankment hid the orchard from his house.

It was general practice on rural lines to collect bean or pea sticks from hedgerows or dig a briar, trim it, stick it through the water-hole in the tender to keep it fresh until he could take it home and bud it.

Keep to the Rules

Railway rule books provide fascinating reading, the 1856 Taff Vale issue proving no exception.

> All persons, especially those in uniform, are to keep their hair cut. Every person is to come on duty daily, clean in his person and clothes, shaved and his boots blacked.
>
> It is urgently requires every person ... on Sundays and Holy Days when he is not required on duty, that he will attend a place of worship, as it will be the means of promotion when vacancies occur.

On the back cover of the Somerset & Dorset Railway working timetables were printed short homilies for their servants. One read:

A driver of a bank engine and his fireman were suspended for one week for allowing a train to leave Shepton without them and then following at great speed, running into and damaging the van.

Another was:

A fireman has been fined for ejecting water over a Station Agent [the S & D term for a stationmaster].

Listen Carefully

The secretary of the photographic section of the Public Relations & Publicity Department, Southern Region, British Railways, took a telephone message from Clapham Junction; 'Line out of gauge. Send photographer.'

A photographer was duly sent and found to his consternation that the message really was: 'Lion out of cage. Send photographer.'

A lion had escaped from a circus in transit and was strolling about the station to the alarm of both passengers and staff. It was eventually recaptured.

3

Stations

A simple station on a single track line had one platform used by both Up and Down trains, so it followed that a double track station should have two platforms, one on the Up line and one on the Down. Although normally the platforms were opposite, sometimes they were staggered, this being particularly useful when adjacent to a level crossing. This meant that the platform could be placed beyond the crossing, allowing the gates to be opened to road traffic immediately behind the train.

Isambard Kingdom Brunel, with his fresh thinking, believed that if a town was situated on just one side of a railway, in order to avoid passengers having to cross a line to reach a platform, two stations should be built on the line nearest the town, an Up station and a Down station. Logically the Up station was at the Up end of the layout and the Down station at the other end. The design also had the advantage that luggage did not need to cross the rails and non-stop trains could run clear of the platforms.

Although this was a splendid idea in the early days when the train service was relatively sparse, as the train service grew more dense, the fact of a train having to cross to another line caused delays and when trains became longer, the original platforms proved too short so what had been two platforms was made into one and a new platform built for the other line. Brunel had one-sided stations at Reading, Taunton, Exeter and Gloucester.

45. A rural station, with two platforms.

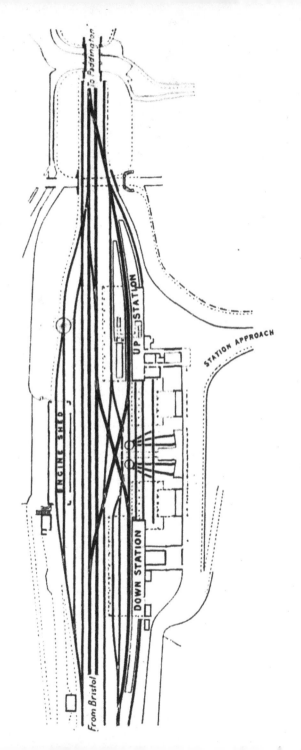

46. Plan of Brunel's one-sided station at Reading.

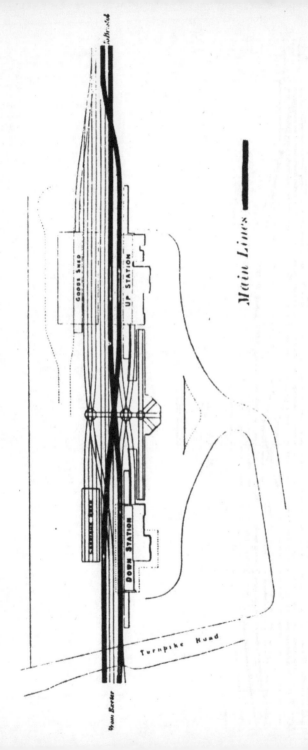

47. Plan of Brunel's one-sided station at Taunton.

Main Lines ▬▬▬▬

The Great Eastern Railway station at Cambridge still retains its long single platform.

Some stations with a very long platform had a crossover midway allowing it to be used by two shorter trains, the crossover permitting the rear train to leave before the forward one.

If an under- or an over-line bridge was in the vicinity of a station, and if that station was on a double track line, it was more economic to construct and maintain it if it was designed as an island platform set between the Up and Down roads, with the bridge providing access. If it was a small station with only very few staff, ticket control was easier because there was only one entrance, whereas with a station with an Up and a Down platform there were often two and this could be a problem if two trains arrived simultaneously. The Great Central Railway was a proponent of this design. Island platforms were also used when a station required extension, access generally being by a footbridge or a subway.

Another platform design was the bay platform. This was a terminal platform set alongside a through platform, or cut into the end of a wide island platform. At junction stations trains starting or terminating often used a bay platform.

The early termini usually had an arrival platform and a departure platform with carriage sidings in between. Large termini were often 'open' stations which aided passengers stepping from coaches into horse-drawn carriages or cabs. In order to check tickets at these open stations before arriving, trains called at a ticket platform. Not used by the public, it was a simple platform where collectors could inspect tickets. Sometimes instead of building a special platform, an existing station just prior to a terminus was used for inspection.

In the early days, stations did not always have specially dedicated buildings. Eton College, afraid of the influence the railway might have on its pupils, had a clause inserted in the Great

49. The GWR station at Paddington.

48. The concourse at Paddington known as 'The Lawn'.

Western Railway Act preventing the construction of a station, without the consent of the provost and fellows, within 3 miles of the school. The Great Western Railway easily circumvented this clause by merely stopping at the nearby Slough to pick up or deposit passengers, and not actually having a station, passengers purchased railway tickets at the nearby Crown Inn.

The provost and fellows applied to the Court of Chancery to halt this invasion of the Act, but their application was dismissed with costs. Curiously, within a month of their defeat, the college chartered a special train to convey its pupils to London for Queen Victoria's Coronation in 1838. A station was opened at Slough in June 1840.

Sometimes existing buildings for a station, such as in 1884 when an extension was built from Bridport to the harbour at West Bay, a thatched cottage at East Street, Bridport was economically converted to a combined stationmaster's house, booking office and waiting room. Surprisingly the roof did not catch alight, but perhaps wisely, the GWR replaced it with a standard design brick station and stationmaster's house. The Stockton & Darlington Railway used a converted warehouse for a station at Darlington, while in 1832 the Leicester & Swannington railway initially just hired a room in the Ashby Road Hotel as a booking office, but later purchased the whole building.

Sloane Square underground station was built with two flights of stairs instead of only one and was double the depth of other District Railway stations. This was because the railway needed to pass under the River Tyburn which was carried above the railway in a huge pipe.

Bank station on the City & South London Railway lay beneath the Church of St Mary Woolnoth.

The platforms at St Pancras were only the top part of the station, the basement being used for the storage of an enormous number of barrels of Burton beer. The supporting columns were located so that the maximum number of barrels could be placed between them. This basement is now used as the Eurostar reception area.

Sometimes a railway company had to build a public station due to the demands of a landowner. In return for permission to run its line through 3½ miles of the Duke of Beaufort's estate, the GWR agreed to give the Duke and his successors the right to stop any train at Badminton station. As this proved to be inconvenient for the working population, British Railways attempted to end this agreement in Parliament in 1963. However, they were unsuccessful. With the exception of Badminton, all stations on the line were closed to passenger traffic when the local service between Bristol and Swindon was withdrawn in April 1961, but five expresses continued to call at Badminton until 3 June 1968 when BR succeeded in having its obligation abolished.

Other landowners sometimes imposed different restrictions. Squire Gordon, of Kemble, Gloucestershire hated the idea of the Swindon to Gloucester line spoiling his view and insisted that the line in the vicinity of his house be placed in a tunnel 415 yards in length. Built by the cut-and-cover method, its two headings were misaligned by about a foot. From December 1995 it was no longer classified as a tunnel but an overbridge, yet remaining as a tunnel for inspection purposes.

Private Stations

If a landowner wanted a station and the railway company did not provide one, it was possible to have a private station, an example being Black Dog on the Chippenham to Calne branch. This was paid for by the Marquess of Lansdowne, but he allowed the public to use it. The Marquess paid a portion of the stationmaster's salary and provided him with a house and 4 tons of coal annually. It became a public station on 15 September 1952. Until that date, the halt did not exist for ticket purposes, for Down passengers for Black Dog booked to Calne for the station beyond, or for Up passengers from Calne to Stanley Bridge.

The fact that Black Dog did not appear in timetables caused problems to strangers because Stanley Bridge Halt was the only published intermediate stop – if counting the stations they thought that Black Dog must be Calne.

On Saturday evenings during the Second World War there were usually many servicemen on the last train from Chippenham and it was common practice for it not to make the scheduled call at Black Dog Halt on the Down journey. This was because members of the armed forces, who were the worse for drink, would alight thinking it was Calne and the guard would then experience difficulty in getting them back on board again. To avoid this problem, it was the custom to tell local residents who wanted to get off at Black Dog that they would be carried through to Calne and dropped off on the return to Chippenham.

50. A Black Dog Siding to Chippenham ticket.

The Calne branch was unusual in that although only 5½ miles long, it was worked by engines from no less than four sheds: Bath, Bristol, Chippenham and Westbury.

In the Scottish Highlands, 86 miles north of Inverness, was Dunrobin. The LMS timetables showed it as 'Dunrobin (Private)'. A station on the Duke of Sutherland's estate – a train would only stop for a guest or an employee.

Including stations on hospital, industrial and military railways, there were about 1,600 private stations.

The Height of Platforms

As early carriages had step boards, access to them from ground level, or a low platform, was easy for the able-bodied. In due course platforms were raised towards the height of a carriage floor. This meant that at some stations the platforms sloped downwards from platform edge to the station building.

The minimum requirement for a station was a booking office, lamp room, waiting room or shelter and ladies' and gentlemen's lavatories. Often there was a stationmaster's office, a parcels and left-luggage office, while larger stations had a refreshment room and a ladies' room and perhaps first, second and third class waiting rooms.

Ticket Office and Tickets

Waiting rooms were heated in the winter and were made more cheerful by posters and photographs of places served by rail. Some waiting rooms where the staff were particularly attentive could have plants and even books and magazines. Recycling is no new notion. In 1867 a box to collect newspapers, books and magazines discarded by passengers was fixed to each of the platforms at Bath so that the literature could be used by patients of the Royal United and Mineral Water Hospitals. Similar schemes operated at other stations.

Desecration of the Bible

Quite a number of stations were given Bibles to place in their waiting rooms, though whether these have furthered the Christian cause may perhaps be questioned.

In 1864 the writer of a letter to the *Bath Chronicle* saw two children and their mother leaving the waiting room. 'On her leaving the room, I discovered that she had been sitting upon an open copy of the Holy Bible. Within the leaves was part of a slice of bread, which one of the children had been eating. Now I question the propriety of placing the sacred volume in such a situation. It is calculated to procure neither piety nor reverence.'

Signal boxes also often had a copy of the Bible and many a lonely signalman, alone in the dead of night, received comfort from reading it.

A Cathedral Controls Shunting Operations

Sometimes a church controlled shunting operations. No, the dean was not to be seen uncoupling wagons, but at Canon's Marsh Goods Depot, Bristol, working instructions stated that shunting must be suspended during the hours of service in the nearby Bristol Cathedral.

In the film *The Titfield Thunderbolt* a bishop helped to run a branch line and, although this was fiction, it certainly is a fact that many of the clergy and church organists are fascinated by railways. At Cadeby, Leicestershire, the vicar had a splendid two-foot gauge railway in his garden and gave his churchwardens rides after Matins.

The Longest Station Name

The Welsh village in Anglesey served by the LMS used the abbreviated name Llanfair for many years, but as a publicity stunt the LMS erected a banner 25 foot long with its title in full: Llanfairpwllgwyngyllgogerychwyrndrobwllllantysiliogogogoch.

Train Sheds: Advantages and Disadvantages

In the early Victorian era towns of importance felt that they should be given a train shed – a roof spanning both platforms and intermediate lines. It was not always of practical advantage as the supporting columns of the train sheds at Bath and Bristol were so close to the platform edge that detraining passengers were likely to bump into them. As the mudguards over the large diameter broad gauge wheels protruded through a carriage floor just by the exit, passengers tripped over these and went flying head-first into these pillars.

Stations and Population

Southport, with a population in the 1930s of 80,000, was served by no fewer than sixteen stations.

51. A platform ticket for Llanfairpwllgwyngyllgogerychwyrndrobwllllantysiliogogogoch.

The Unfortunate Result of Dining at Swindon

Swindon station was built free by the contractors, with the GWR undertaking to stop all passenger trains at Swindon for ten minutes, no other stop for refreshment being allowed between London and Bristol, the idea being that the contractor would recoup his outlay in catering profits.

The GWR was not always very punctilious in the time it spent at Swindon and trains were sometimes started again after a stop of only seven or eight minutes. On 7 August 1891 Mr Lowenfield caught the 3.00 p.m. train at Paddington with a first class ticket to Teignmouth. The train was timed to arrive at Swindon at 4.27 p.m. and booked to leave again at 4.37 p.m.

Since he was not due to reach Teignmouth till 7.42 p.m, Mr Lowenfield somewhat rashly perhaps, elected to take an early dinner during the Swindon stop. It may be that he demolished the peculiar fare, which Swindon dignified with the name of dinner, in eight minutes. If so, the Great Western was too fast for him, for the train only waited seven minutes and when a presumably replete Mr Lowenfield stepped on to the platform, it had gone.

Mr Lowenfield, of course, was furious. There was no further connection to Teignmouth for another four hours and, even on an August evening, there were perhaps few who would enjoy Swindon for that length of time. He accordingly decided to catch the next train to Bristol and ordered by telegraph a special train to be ready to convey him from Bristol to Teignmouth.

Mr Lowenfield's special may have been the very last to run over the broad gauge which finished in May 1892. It cost him £37 17s 0d and he paid this sum by cheque to the Bristol stationmaster, but the next morning stopped it.

The GWR brought an action for the recovery from Mr Lowenfield of the cost of the special train. He responded with a

52. Swindon station *c.* 1850.

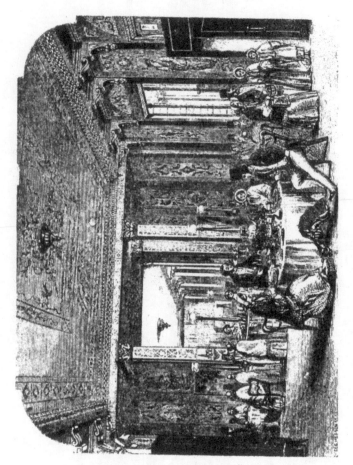

53. The first class refreshment room at Swindon *c.* 1850.

counter-claim for damages, on the grounds that the railway had failed to carry him to Teignmouth and had broken its contract by not stopping at Swindon for the stipulated ten minutes.

The judge agreed that the passenger was entitled to damages on account of the premature start of the train from Swindon, which he assessed at forty shillings and he was also entitled to a refund of the first class fare between Bristol and Teignmouth and to the reimbursement of three shillings spent on telegrams to an anxious family. The judge did not agree, however, that the suffering which would have been caused to Mr Lowenfield and his family was such that he was justified in ordering a special. The Great Western Railway was therefore granted the recovery of the cost of the special and also the full costs of the action.

No Building Regulations

About 2.30 a.m. on 26 March 1898, men in the Swindon yard observed what they thought was a chimney fire in the hotel on the Up platform. Every fireplace in the building was examined and found to be in order. It was then noticed that flames were coming from the roof. Twenty female bar attendants and maid servants were evacuated from their quarters on the upper floor, the last man to leave the building being the man who was the solitary guest, though the previous night a large number of men had been staying there.

The Swindon Fire Brigade arrived at 3.50 a.m. and the GWR fire engine ten minutes later. The fire was under control at 5.55 a.m., but the block was gutted. Traffic on the Up line was suspended as some of the walls had become dangerously weak and required demolition. Men on the night shift in the part of the Works nearest the station flocked to aid the station staff and firemen. Liquour was removed to safety and drinking indulged in, officials as well as rank and file becoming tipsy.

Charles Kislingbury, Divisional Superintendent, Bristol, received news at his home just before 5.00 a.m. He left Bristol Temple Meads by special train at 6.15 a.m., the locomotive and single coach arriving at Swindon at 7.00 a.m. giving an average speed of about 60 mph.

What caused the fire? The chimney was Z-shaped and although swept a fortnight before, its shape encouraged lodgement of soot, but more serious was the fact that a timber beam ran across the chimney. Circumstances which led to the fire's rapid spread was the fact that a gale was blowing, the interior walls were lath and plaster and the incredible system of running lead gas pipes down the flues.

Station in a Tree Trunk

Probably the most curious English station was that at Moreton-on-Lugg on the Shrewsbury & Hereford Railway just north of Hereford, and which was opened on 6 December 1853. For some time after the opening of the line, the station there was in a large tree trunk!

The Shrewsbury & Hereford Railway was very particular in the selection of its servants as every candidate for a post was subjected to a deep inquiry into his character and antecedents before he was eligible for consideration.

Halts and Platforms

Early in the twentieth century, railways began to feel rivalry from electric trams and motor buses which usually ran much closer to passengers' homes. To combat this competition railways opened halts, some just a stopping place without a platform, but when traffic developed, a simple platform would be erected having a

54. An oak tree used as a railway station at Moreton-on-Lugg.

shelter, but no other facilities. Often the platform surface was made from old sleepers, but these had the disadvantage of becoming slippery in wet weather. In the late 1950s, many were replaced with concrete structures, only to be made redundant by the Beeching cuts. Sometimes a concrete platform from a closed branch would replace a timber platform on a still open line. As halts were unstaffed, tickets could be obtained from a nearby house, public house, or from a conductor-guard.

One particularly unusual halt was on the Kemble to Tetbury branch in Gloucestershire. To combat road competition and enable the branch to be worked more economically, the Western Region introduced four-wheeled railbuses on 2 February 1959. To open the line to a wider market, two new halts were opened, one was at Trouble House and had the honour of being the only halt in the country just serving an inn. These new halts were cheap to construct being merely wooden boards at rail level and about 10 square feet. Although the railbus, with a more

55. Ticket issued on a GWR steam rail motor serving halts in the Forest of Dean.

intensive timetable, increased traffic by as much as 150 per cent, the branch closed on 6 April 1964. It was hoped to run through services over the main line between Kemble and Swindon, but the vehicles' light weight was insufficient to operate a track circuit, so they were only permitted to run empty over the main line to Swindon where they were serviced and refuelled every other day.

Well-used halts sometimes became a 'Platform', that is a halt which was staffed for at least part of the day. Over the last thirty years or so the term 'halt' and 'platform' have fallen out of use and today many small wayside stations are halts, though this does not actually appear in their name.

Hospital and Other Special Stations

Hampshire had two hospital stations. On 19 May 1856 Queen Victoria laid the foundation stone of the Royal Victoria Hospital, Netley, to accommodate military patients, initially from the Crimean War. A special hospital platform was provided at Netley, but as the hospital was nearly three-quarters of a mile from the station, this was far from satisfactory. In 1899 the War Department asked the London & South Western Railway to lay a branch to the hospital. It opened 18 April 1900 and the 196-foot-long covered platform was connected to the hospital by a covered way. The small ticket office was manned, when required, by Netley station staff. The hospital's steam supply was able to warm coaches before use. Between 24 August 1914 and 31 December 1918 approximately 1,200 hospital trains used Netley. As the line fell at 1 in 70 towards the hospital, outgoing trains sometimes lost adhesion, particularly in autumn when the rails were damp and covered with leaves from overhanging trees. On some occasions the trip up to the main line could take as long as forty-five minutes. In June and July 1944 up to five fourteen-to-sixteen coach trains left Netley Hospital daily with an engine at each end. The last train over the line ran on 30 August 1955 and both hospital and station were demolished in 1967. The strangest train to use the station was in 1942 when K10 4-4-0 No. 142 arrived with about twenty horseboxes whose occupants had been bombed out and had been brought to enjoy the grass in the hospital grounds.

The other hospital station in Hampshire was near Butts Junction, Alton, where a line was laid to a hospital and convalescent camp with accommodation for 500 men, built under the auspices of the delightfully named Absent Minded Beggar Fund. This curious title came from the fact that at fundraising concerts for the construction of the hospital during the South African War, Rudyard Kipling's poem 'The Absent Minded Beggar' was recited. The line was eventually lifted, but a similar one opened on 5 April 1910 for the Lord Mayor Treloar's Cripples' Home which received 1,500 tons of coal annually. A 200-foot-long platform was situated on the Basingstoke to Alton branch and used by Founder's Day specials.

Industrial stations could be very varied from Acrow Halt, Saffron Waldon, Ampress Works Halt, Lymington, Daimler Halt, Coventry; Salvation Army Halt, St Albans serving a printing works; to Singer Works Platform, Clydeside, while there were many stations for miners situated in the various coalfields.

Apart from stations on a military railway, the forces had stations at such varied places as Barry Review Platform, Angus; Britannia Halt for the Royal Naval College, Dartmouth; Kidwelly Flats Halt, South Wales; and Lympstone Commando, near Exmouth.

Railways had special platforms for some of their employees such as Barassie Workshops, Glasgow & South Western Railway, Caerphilly Works on the Rhymney Railway. There were also platforms for the convenience of railway families, such as

Meldon Quarry Halt in Devon, Hoo Junction in Kent and Sugar Loaf Summit on the Central Wales line.

It is a little-known fact that the present Southampton Airport station is on the site of the Atlantic Park Hostel Halt, which served as a reception centre for emigrants to America. The 3 foot gauge Isle of Man Railway could boast of three private stations: Bishop's Court Halt for the Bishop of Sodor and Man; Braddan Halt for those attending the open-air church services and Quarter Bridge for motorcycle race spectators.

Railways & Local Taxation

It is not generally realised that in many rural and semi-rural districts the railways paid the largest share of local taxation, frequently being as much as 70–90 per cent. In 1920 the GWR paid the largest amount of any railway company, namely £1,425,274, followed by the London & North Western at £1,328,645, the North Eastern £1,071,793 and the Midland £1,012,019.

There's Always Hope

In 1955 a passenger anxious to travel to Aycliffe was told at a London terminal enquiry office that the station was closed, but failed to fully comprehend what this meant.

The helpful clerk started looking up buses from Darlington and presented the enquirer with the results. The latter was still unhappy because he wanted to travel by train, not by bus. 'But the station is *closed*,' repeated the clerk.

At last comprehension dawned: 'Ah, yes, I see, closed ... yes. Well when does it open?'

Stroud Station Adopts a Tree

Stroud station in Gloucestershire has an American beech tree on its Down platform. When the station opened in 1845 there was a plantation of trees and shrubs at the rear of the Down platform. Untouched at first, as traffic requirements grew, trees had to be felled to make room for new buildings. Alterations to the station in 1890 included extensions to the platform, but this American beech was left standing just behind the platform railings. It formed a welcome shade on a hot day and a seat was placed to take advantage of the tree's shelter. Extensions in 1913–14 included shifting the fence, so brought the tree on the platform itself.

At this time its future was in the balance and there was much talk of felling the tree to create more space. People appealed and it was spared, a seat being built right round the trunk. During the Second World War the United States' troops collected seeds to take 'back home' and plant as a momento. It is an American fern leaf beech tree, *polypodum phegopteris*, uncommon in this country and now about 170 years old.

The Kiddies' Express

Children had a hard time during the Second World War with no metal toys being made; sweets on ration and travel curtailed. In August 1946 the GWR decided, with the restoration of cheap day fares, to run the first post-war excursion from London just for children. With the enthusiastic cooperation of Weston-super-Mare plans were laid for a trip to that resort.

As soon as news of the project appeared in the press, applications poured in and a week before the chosen date, the fixed number of 500 available tickets for children and parents had been sold.

The train consisted of eleven vehicles plus a generator van appropriately headed by 4-6-0 No. 1004 *County of Somerset*. The leading and rear vans had been transformed into miniature theatres with raised and lighted stages. Musical clowns performed in the front van and a magician and a piano-accordionist at the rear. As there were three performances before arriving at Weston, there was time to see both shows. A buffet car was provided to offer refreshments. Puzzles were handed to the older children.

A band of girl pipers welcomed the train at Locking Road station and a donkey carriage resembling a locomotive drew alongside *County of Somerset*. As the children left the train they found, not a taxi rank, but a fleet of donkey carts to parade them through the town.

The children enjoyed seven hours by the sea with a treasure hunt on the sands; singing and whistling contests at the Rozel bandstand, with several children conducting the orchestra; free admission to the Grand Pier, the Marine Lake and other attractions.

Only one child made no compliments regarding the arrangements for he slept most of the time, but Peter, the youngest tripper, was only five weeks old.

Down Station on the Main Line and the Up Station on a Spur

Until relatively recently the station layout at Dorchester was most peculiar: the Down platform was on the main line, but Up trains had to back into the Up platform placed on a spur.

This curious situation arose because the original station of the Southampton & Dorchester Railway was a terminus, but when the extension to Weymouth was made, it was not found practicable to extend the tracks beyond the terminus. The

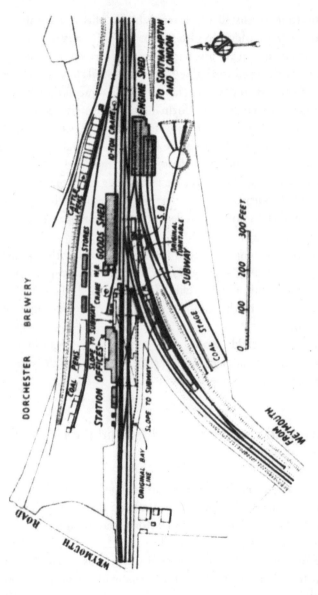

56. Track layout at Dorchester, showing the Up platform on a spur.

through line, branching southwards just short of the terminus was given a Down platform, but one was not provided for Up trains. This meant that all Up passenger trains had to clear the junction and then set back into the original terminus on which the main station offices were situated. Access from the town was to the Up platform which was connected to the Down platform by a subway.

This manoeuvre cost a minute and the construction of a Down platform only required the removal of one signal and the abandonment of a small area of railwaymen's Brussels sprouts.

Time Zones

Even in the relatively small country of Great Britain there is a considerable discrepancy which exists between Greenwich Mean Time and local time: thirty-one minutes vanished under the influence of longitude on a journey from Penzance to Walton-on-the-Naze. A journey by stagecoach spread the time loss over several days, but the advent of railways reduced this to just a few hours.

Even when railway time was adopted and uniformity instilled by regulating railway station clocks to London time, innate conservatism resulted in the fitting of two hands to certain village church timepieces in order to mark both the railway and local reckonings.

Quite a few passengers, not possessing clocks, went by the sun, and those living west of Greenwich not infrequently forgot to make due allowance for the difference and arrived at the station to see their train disappearing.

The original length of the GWR from London to Bristol spanned two degrees, thirty-three minutes of longitude, involving a time difference of eleven minutes. So of the early railway companies, the GWR was the most inconvenienced by local time difference as most of the other major railways tended to run north to south. When the Bristol & Exeter Railway came on the scene, on 30 July 1841 the GWR issued a through timetable stating:

London Time is kept at all the stations on the railway, which is about 4 minutes earlier than the Reading time; 5½ minutes before Steventon time; 7½ minutes before Cirencester time; 8 minutes before Chippenham time; 11 minutes before Bath and Bristol ; and 14 minutes before Bridgewater time.

In the early days of railways, solar time as shown by the local sundial provided the basis of ascertaining London time, but during 1852, telegraph wires were laid along the GWR system and an order dated 20 October 1852 read:

Commencing on November 1st, the hourly signals will be transmitted regularly at stated times, and the operators are warned to keep the lines clear for two minutes preceding the hour and to watch for the signal to check the station clocks. You are at liberty to allow local clock and watch makers to have Greenwich time, providing such liberty shall not interfere with the Company's services, etc.

It was not until 1880 that the British Parliament followed the lead of the railways and enacted that the word 'time' for legal purposes, when relating to Great Britain, should imply Greenwich Mean Time.

Special Exits from Stations

Great Malvern has a splendid station designed by E. M. Elmslie who additionally designed its environs; the landscaped approach road and gardens, the road bridge and Imperial Hotel, now Malvern Girls' College. An unusual feature was a special subway direct from the Down platform into the adjacent hotel. At one time there was a siding at the Up end of the Down platform to enable trucks of coal to be taken through a tunnel parallel with the pedestrian subway to the hotel, and later college, boiler room. This siding was taken out of use on 21 October 1956. At least until 1959 water from the college was supplied by the railway from pumps in Malvern tunnel.

Westminster on the District Railway had its special corridor so that MPs and Peers could walk into the Houses of Parliament without having to cross the street. Leicester Square tube station had a corridor leading directly into the vestibule of the London Hippodrome and there is a long passage from South Kensington station into the museums. During the First World War it was used for the storage of museum valuables against the threat of bombs during air raids.

From 1845 until 26 January 1936 an open girder footbridge offered a direct connection between the Up platform of the GWR's Bath station and the Royal Hotel, built by Chadwick, the railway contractor, on the opposite side of the street. Giuseppe Garibaldi, the Italian patriot and hero, planned to address Bath citizens from this bridge, but the crowd of dignitaries greeting his train prevented him from leaving the coach.

A further interesting fact about Bath station is that in 1895 it was one of the first in the country to be lit by electricity; even until the 1960s many stations were lit by oil or gas. Initially the GWR had its own generating plant, but in 1902 found it cheaper to purchase power from the City Corporation's generating station next door. Until 1953 railway coal wagons for the generating station were horse-drawn. This was because, due to the cramped situation, wagons had to be turned at right angles on a turntable. On one occasion the horse fell over a low wall on to the roof of a building below track level, the animal landing with its hoofs in the air. Fortunately the fire brigade was able to retrieve it unharmed.

An Artful Porter

Manchester London Road station had a long approach with a subtle, but telling gradient, almost specifically designed for the benefit of outside porters. An old hand at the game had more sense than to offer his services at the foot of the slope, but waited until his potential client had already completed half the job. This meant that the porter did not have as far to carry the luggage and the client was more willing to accept help.

Peculiarities at Stations

Due to geography, some stations had peculiarities. At Exeter St David's and Plymouth North Road, SR and GWR trains to London travelled in opposite directions, while at Birmingham New Street both the Up and Down Pines Express used the same platform and travelled in the same direction.

The Fort Augustus Branch

The Fort Augustus branch of the North British Railway from Spean Bridge to Fort Augustus lost its passenger service on 1

FORT-AUGUSTUS and SPEAN BRIDGE.—Invergarry and Fort-Augustus.—North British.						
Mls		mrn	aft	aft	Thurs	Mons
	Fort-Augustus ....dep.	8 30	Wed 2 30	Tues 7 15		
4½	Aberchalder	8 39	2 42	7 27		
9	Invergarry	8 51	2 56	7 41		
13½	Invergloy Platform	Sig.	8 Sig.	8 Sig.		
18¼	Gairlochy	9 17	3 33	8 18		
24	Spean Bridge *(above)* arr.	9 25	3 45	8 30		

Mls		mrn	aft	aft	Thurs	Mons
2½	Spean Bridge ....dep.	1025	Wed 4 10	9 15		
7½	Gairlochy	1033	4 22	9 27		
15	Invergloy Platform	Sig.	8 Sig.	8 Sig.		
19½	Invergarry	1059	4 59	10 4		
23	Aberchalder	1111	5 18	1018		
24	Fort-Augustus ....arr.	1120	5 25	1090		

57. The Fort Augustus branch timetable for April 1910.

December 1933, following which there was only one train per week. This left Spean Bridge on Saturdays with only coal and petrol, while all other traffic was dealt with by LNER motor-lorries and David McBrayne's buses and steamers, the latter in the summer only.

The first station was Gairlochy where the guard's wife was station-mistress, an unusual appointment for a female in the 1930s. Part of the station buildings was converted into a camping hostel, similar to a camp coach, but with fireplaces, a telephone and water laid on. Similar arrangements were made at Invergarry and Fort Augustus, the charge averaging £2 to £3 per person per week. The branch closed entirely on 1 January 1947.

Long Railway Mileage in Twenty-Four Hours

In August 1923 it was possible to cover 1,120.5 miles in twenty-four hours, the itinerary being:

From	At	To	Arrive	Distance (miles)
	a.m.		a.m.	
Berwick	12.03	King's Cross	7.05	335.5
King's Cross	7.15	Grantham	9.23	105.2
Grantham	9.36	King's Cross	11.30	105.2
King's Cross	11.50	York	(p.m.) 3.20	188.2
	p.m.		p.m.	
York	4.00	King's Cross	7.30	188.2
King's Cross	7.38	Wood Green	7.49	5
Wood Green	7.51	King's Cross	8.10	5
King's Cross	8.20	York	11.55	188.2
			Total	1,120½

Free Boot Cleaning at Morden Station

In 1930 two automatic boot-cleaning machines were installed at Morden station on the Bakerloo line so that passengers could clean their boots free of charge. The innovation was due to the large quantity of mud which had been carried to the station by workmen employed on neighbouring building estates, but the appliances were also available for use by other passengers. The machines were placed between the ticket barrier and the platform.

Stations Without Railway Tracks

One of the GWR's claims for being different was that for eighty-seven years it had a station to which no rails were ever laid. Dartmouth station had a fine cast-iron crest to its slate roof, and a glazed and valance canopy on its road side. It was not directly opposite the railway station at Kingswear, but several hundred yards upstream. Due to the Royal Naval College traffic, for many years the stationmaster at Dartmouth was of a higher grade than his colleague at Kingswear – despite not having any trains!

This was not the first rail-less GWR station. A station was built at Bradford-on-Avon in 1848, but due to the aftermath of the Railway Mania investors were reluctant to purchase shares and much to the disgust of the townsfolk, the track was not actually laid for nine years!

A Holiday Record

A remarkably brisk turnaround of a train took place at Hastings one Saturday in August 1939. A train of nine bogie coaches arrived late from London, was emptied of passengers and holiday luggage, hastily cleaned and refilled with a fresh complement of passengers and luggage for Charing Cross. A fresh Schools class 4-4-0 replaced the one which had brought the train down and all this work was carried out in four minutes thirteen seconds.

At an evening rush hour the same station handled fifteen passenger trains in forty-five minutes at its two island platforms having a total of four tracks. They comprised six electric trains and nine steam-hauled trains.

The Wrong Turning

It is very unusual for a train to take the wrong line. One instance occurred on 8 August 1940 when an Inner Circle train of the London Transport Passenger Board arrived on the electric side of the GWR station at Paddington. The mistake was due to the signalman at Edgware Road giving the train the wrong line at the junction, though it was surprising that the motorman failed to spot this when he saw the junction signals. At Paddington the train was taken over the crossover to the Up line and returned to Edgware Road where it was again reversed, and then it proceeded to its correct route.

Movable Platforms

One of the characteristics of British railways has been the provision of platforms, now normally 3 feet 1½ inches above rail level, but in past times it was lower. Platforms enable passengers to board carriages at floor level rather than to climb up from the ground as is the practice in many continental countries.

Normally a British platform is fixed, but in a few locations, considerations of space have resulted in the adoption of a

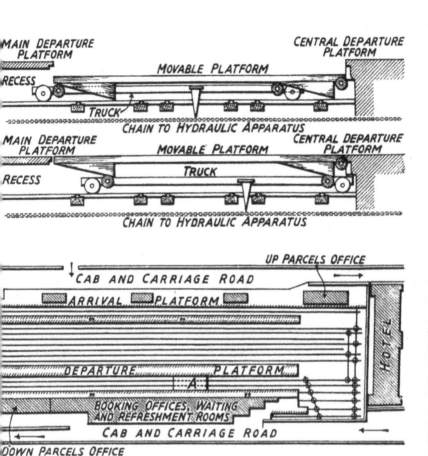

58. The arrangement of the movable connection between the two departure platforms at Paddington in 1878.

movable section. An outstanding instance was where the Paddington terminus, built by Brunel, had one main departure platform and one arrival platform, the two being separated by five storage roads. In addition there were two subsidiary departure lines served by an island platform which had no permanent connection with the 'mainland' as the present concourse was occupied by small turntables to transfer rolling stock from one road to another. The island platform could only be accessed by a movable platform supported on a dwarf truck, which, when required, was drawn out by hydraulic machinery from beneath the main departure platform and rose to the same level as the main platforms, becoming a bridge across the rails and giving access to the second departure platform.

The use of the movable platform enabled three long trains to be loaded at once, though the two trains nearest the booking office had to be temporarily divided. When it was necessary to despatch these trains, the movable cross platform was run back to its position beneath the main platform, the first half of the train backed and coupled to the second half.

Another London terminus which had a section of movable platform was the London & South Western Railway's station Waterloo. When the London Bridge to Waterloo Junction extension of the South Eastern Railway was opened on 11 January 1864, a connection was made with the LSWR by a single line which crossed Waterloo Road on a bridge, ran across what is now the circulating area of the main Waterloo station and joined the middle road between platform roads No. 4 and No. 5.

As this link was only used occasionally, when it was out of use a section of movable platform was placed in position to allow passengers and luggage to cross the connecting line at platform level. The connecting line and movable platform were abolished in the course of the station rebuilding which was completed in 1922.

Prior to the time when the Metropolitan Railway's Baker Street station was rebuilt, a movable platform gave access from platform one to platforms two and three across a single line which provided a physical connection between the Circle and the St John's Wood lines.

This movable platform was a four-wheel truck which ran into a short siding in the connecting tunnel when a train was required to pass over the line. It was replaced in 1911 when the connecting line was doubled by a form of drawbridge, which was then abolished in 1913 on the completion of new overhead access between the platforms.

Saxmundham and Halesworth stations on the Yarmouth line had their platforms intersected by road level crossings. The crossing gates were designed to have a platform so that when closed to road traffic they could connect up both sections of the platform.

Other stations, such as Brockenhurst, have movable platforms which can be swung at a right angle across a line to enable luggage or milk churns to be taken on the level from one platform across to another.

Rare Stops

Some stations had curious timetables. Blunsdon station between Cricklade and Swindon was closed in the autumn of 1924. In its last years, the only trains which called there were in the Down direction and were only on Sundays – of all days!

Got a Light?

About 1900 a workman digging a well shaft at Heathfield, Sussex, found the shaft alight when he threw a match down it.

Subsequently for several years the London, Brighton & South Coast Railway station and nearby houses were lit by this natural gas.

A Turntable Gets Out of Control

Garsdale station on the Settle & Carlisle line is situated high among the Pennines, over 1,100 feet above sea level, and is the highest main line station in England. On one occasion when an engine was being turned in a gale, the wind blew the turntable round and round to the consternation of the railway staff. To prevent a recurrence, a fence of sleepers was erected around the turntable to give shelter.

A Station with a Different Kind of Service

One expects a station to have a train service, but Masbury station, high on the Mendip Hills, also had a different one.

At one time the stationmaster in charge was an ardent Wesleyan and as there was no chapel nearby, on Sundays he held religious services in the waiting room, accompanied by a harmonium.

Another curiosity of the station was that above the bay window of the station house was a carving of Maesbury Castle, which was medieval-looking in its design. Apparently the sculptor was unaware that the real castle was an ancient British encampment.

In the 1930s the Vicar of Barkingside held services in the waiting room of Hainault station on the LNER, while in the 1950s the Vicar of Ingleton held monthly Evensong in the booking hall of Horton station on the Settle & Carlisle line.

Sometimes services actually took place on trains. During the First World War, W. T. Row, a Baptist, conducted services on the trains which ran on the Liverpool Street to Enfield line, while going to and from his City office. He would give an address to passengers, offer prayers and lead in the singing of hymns. The second and third class compartments had partitions only half way up and thus several compartments could easily join in the worship.

Railways Recycle Churches

In contrast to railway property being used for religious services, railway companies also used redundant churches for secular purposes.

In 1880 the Severn & Wye Railway purchased 'the iron church at Cheltenham' for £150, transported it to Lydney and until 1924 used it as a carriage shed and also as a locomotive paint shop.

The GWR bought All Saints' Church, Cardiff and converted it into an electricity generating station. In more recent times, British Railways turned an unwanted Methodist church at Swindon into a railway museum.

Alternatively, after the failure of the atmospheric propulsion on the South Devon Railway, Starcross pumping station, an ornate building, was used as a chapel.

A School below a Railway

Several viaducts in the Bath area were put to interesting uses. In 1854 the vicar of St Matthew's, Widcombe, concerned that there was no infants' school in the Dolemeads area of his parish, purchased land from the GWR and in 1855 a school was built partly under and partly against an archway of a railway

59. Widcombe Infants' School, Bath, in 1855. It was partly situated below the GWR viaduct.

viaduct. The arch was lined with ashlar and below the arch was covered with Croggan's patent asphalt felt. A second arch and the adjoining land formed a dry and spacious playground with flower borders and a swing. In 1900 the school moved to a new building on a different site.

West of Bath station one of the arches was used as a mortuary until 1948, while an adjoining arch housed a bakery. Another arch formed a police station and when this closed in April 1923 the premises were taken over by a greengrocer. Yet another arch held a tea and coffee stall.

The construction of Twerton Viaduct, 2 miles west of Bath station, required the demolition of some cottages belonging to the local landowner. They were replaced as an integral part of the viaduct. Each dwelling had two rooms, each with a fireplace. The flue ran horizontally to a chimney designed as a buttress to the outside southern wall of the viaduct. The front room facing the road had a window, but the back room, for sleeping purposes, was without. The houses fell out of use as dwellings, probably in the latter half of the nineteenth century. It is not known why, as vibration and dampness was not a problem. As the cottages on the opposite side of the road were without a garden for drying washing, the cottages under the railway were rented by them for a nominal sum and a coal merchant used two for storing coal. Today they are still in use as industrial storage units or workshops.

4

Track

Why Four Foot Eight and a Half Inches?

Most of the first railways in England were built to the gauge of 4 feet 8½ inches because they were built by the same men who built pre-railway tramways and that was the gauge they used. Those men chose that gauge for the tramways because they used the same jigs and tools that were previously used for building road wagons, and the wagons used that wheel spacing.

If those wagon builders had tried to use any other spacing, the wheel ruts on some of the old roads would have broken the wagon axles, so they had to match the spacing of the wheel ruts worn into those roads. Some of those initial ruts were made by Roman war chariots and since the chariots were made by Roman chariot-makers, they had consistent wheel spacing.

But why did Roman war chariot designers choose a wheel spacing of 4 feet 8½ inches? They chose this spacing because that was the width needed to accommodate the rear end of a Roman warhorse. When you're next in Pompeii, measure the ruts in the road.

A Broad Gauge Mystery

As both the broad gauge GWR and the standard gauge London & South Western Railway wished to reach Weymouth, the GWR agreed to lay an extra rail to form mixed gauge between Dorchester Junction and Weymouth. The GWR agreed to this based on the condition that the LSWR laid broad gauge for 8 miles east of Dorchester, leaving each company with running powers over the mixed gauge section. The importance of access to Weymouth by the LSWR is obvious, but the benefit of the GWR of holding running powers to a point midway between the country stations of Moreton and Wool is a mystery.

Unusual Mixed Gauge Track

Brunel disliked facing points and so devised an ingenious method whereby narrow and broad gauge trains could be sent on diverging paths without the use of ordinary switches controlled from a signal box.

A check rail was placed in front of a fixed switch and guided the vehicles by the backs of their flanges towards the diverging route. The diverging rail with the check rail was at a slightly lower level than the opposite rail, so as to give the diverging vehicles a tendency away from the straight line.

This principle was also used for the automatic sidestepping of standard gauge trains while on broad gauge track. In order that the standard gauge coaches could always come close to a platform on whichever side of the line it happened to be situated, the third rail was deflected inward to the broad gauge rail into which it eventually merged, and on the other side, the wheels were diverted from their position to a new third rail by means of a check rail opposite a fixed switch.

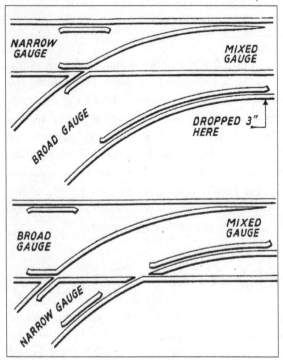

60. Broad and standard gauge fixed points used on the GWR.

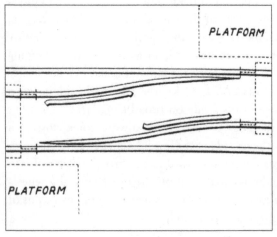

61. The arrangement for sidestepping standard gauge trains running on mixed gauge.

These fixed switches were disliked by Col. Yolland, a Board of Trade Inspector who imposed a speed limit of 8 mph. This was a sensible decision because, in addition to running standard, or broad gauge trains over such a track, November 1871 saw the first GWR mixed train, a goods train between Truro and Penzance consisting of a standard gauge engine followed by standard gauge wagons; then a match truck having a wide buffer width at one end and a standard at the other and fitted with a swivelling coupling hook. Behind it followed broad gauge wagons and a broad gauge brake van.

Variety Is the Spice of Life

Before the Second World War, when railways were at their zenith, there were often quite a few routes to choose from when travelling from A to B. For instance, a timetable clerk arranging to route a train from London Bridge to Deal had no less than 128 fairly direct alternatives from which to choose. Some of the alternatives had little variation from one another, as, for example, the two alternatives: the main line and the Lewisham Junction line between St John's and Hither Green. The majority of the routes were entirely on the Eastern Division, the Central Division only being used for the Tulse Hill and Streatham route to East Croydon.

A Long, Little-Known English Bridge

The Severn Bridge is curious because, although at 4,162 feet in length it was the longest English railway bridge, and in the British Isles third only to those spanning the Tay and the Forth, it was virtually unknown to most people.

62. View downstream to the Severn Bridge, 1879.

63. The Severn Bridge, 1879.

The bridge was built to provide a link with the coalfields of the Forest of Dean and South Wales, to enable ships which had unloaded at Sharpness to coal there and thus avoid the time and expense of sailing to a port on the other side of the Severn estuary.

The bridge was a series of iron bow-string girders resting on cast-iron piers filled with concrete and rock. At its eastern end was a steam-operated swing span across the Gloucester & Berkeley Canal. An engine driver was required to be on duty on one of the day shifts in order to keep the engine and machinery in good order, the signalman on the other shift assisting in cleaning and coaling.

The swing span was left open to shipping at night and also at other times when the railway was not in use, the man on early turn being required to have the engine in steam ready for swinging the span at least twenty minutes before the first train of the day was due. The man on late turn was responsible for banking the fire after the last train had passed and leaving the swing span open. The two boilers were used alternately for a fortnight; one being in use while the other was being washed out.

The bridge opened to traffic on 17 October 1879, intriguingly exactly a century after the very first iron bridge in the world, which was also across the Severn. The very first train to cross the Severn Bridge fired its own twenty-one gun salute, for a detonator had been laid on each of the twenty-one spans.

The opening of the Severn Tunnel in 1886 somewhat eclipsed the value of the bridge, but on winter Sundays when the civil engineer had complete possession of the tunnel, trains were diverted over the bridge.

During the Second World War it was not unknown for pilots on training flights to dive Spitfires and Hurricanes between the bridge deck and the water. An onlooker admired them, until he saw men painting the bridge, hanging in their cradle, while an aircraft flew within feet of them.

On 25 October 1960 the bridge was struck by an oil tanker and two spans were destroyed. Ironically this occurred when the bridge was being strengthened to allow heavier engines across. When BR was faced with a bill of £294,000 for replacing the broken spans, it was decided that repair could not be justified. Unfortunately for BR, under the Merchant Shipping Act the limited liability for damage through collision did not exceed the sum equal to about twenty-four times the net registered tonnage of the vessel, or vessels. BR only received £5,000, while Messrs Fairfield, the contractor for strengthening the bridge, who had lost plant to the value of £10,000, received just a little over £100.

Road-Rail Bridges

An unusual swing bridge could be found on one of the dock sidings at Sharpness. It was designed to carry both a railway and a public road. There was a similar bridge at Connel Ferry but it did not need swinging facilities.

Ashton Swing Bridge at Bristol was interesting as it was had a double deck: a road being on the top level and a double-track railway on the lower level. The hydraulically-worked span measured 202 feet and weighed 1,000 tons. The railway is now closed.

A Telescopic Bridge

The Bridgwater Docks line had a telescopic bridge, rare, but not unique. Officially opened in March 1871, for the first eight months of its life it was worked by manual winches at each end, but then a stationary steam engine was installed.

The bridge was divided into three sections and this sequence was used to open it. The signals at each end were placed at danger and a steel arm set across the rails while gates across the footbridge and the rail track were both locked. Safety precautions having been taken, the bridge's steam engine was started and the gears engaged to move the traversing section sideways on special rails across to its pit. The gears were then changed to drive the chain drum in order to move the main section spanning most of the river, back lengthways into the space vacated by the first section. The third section of the bridge remained fixed.

It is believed that the bridge was not opened after 1953 because the upper berths on the river fell out of use. With shipping usage decreasing as the narrow estuary of the River Parrett was unsuited to modern vessels, the docks branch closed in April 1967.

The First Mixed Gauge Track

Most people believe that the first mixed gauge track appeared on the GWR – this is not so. When the broad gauge Bristol & Gloucester Railway opened on 6 July 1844, the Avon & Gloucestershire Railway with its gauge of 4 feet 8 inches still had the right to use the track between Mangotsfield and Coalpit Heath. The track had been laid by the Bristol & Gloucestershire Railway – a forerunner of the Bristol & Gloucester – so this section of line became the first mixed gauge line in the country. The old fish-bellied rails were laid between the broad gauge rails.

The 4 foot 8 inch gauge line used horses, so as a safety precaution, horse-drawn trains were required to start immediately after a steam-hauled passenger train and these were only allowed to run at intervals of not less than one and a half hours, to ensure that there was no risk of collision.

Timber, Steel or Concrete Sleepers?

In the early days of railways, sleepers were simply stone blocks, even the main line London & Birmingham Railway used this principle. When trains started to run faster, the blocks became dislocated so timber sleepers were almost universally used either transversely or longitudinally under the rails. Of elm or fir, they were treated with a preservative generally forced in under pressure. The standard size was 9 feet long, 10 inches wide and 5 inches deep.

Some railways such as the GWR in the 1930s, experimented with metal sleepers, usually in the form of an inverted steel trough. Rust proved a problem and steel sleepers required to be renewed more frequently than those made of other materials. For secondary routes, modern steel sleepers have much to commend them and 36,400 steel sleepers were installed over 15 miles of the Settle & Carlisle line in 1999. Their shape allows them to be stacked for storage. A sleeper weighs 80 kg and can easily be lifted by two men whereas it takes eight men to lift a concrete sleeper.

With the increasing cost of timber, concrete was tried, but the battering to which a sleeper was subjected was generally too much for the normal reinforced concrete sleeper and it was only with the introduction of pre-stressing methods that concrete sleepers proved reliable. They were however heavier, and more difficult to handle in the days before permanent way maintenance became mechanised. Today the concrete sleeper's heavy weight is now seen as advantageous for holding down long welded rails.

During the Second World War, to conserve supplies of scarce timber, some sidings and branch lines were laid on concrete pots under the chairs, the pots being tied together with iron bars.

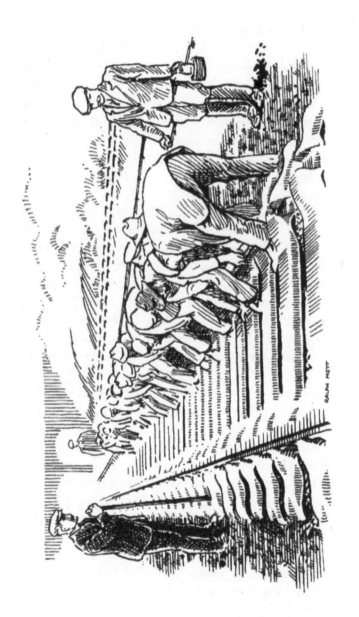

64. Gangers laying steel sleepers on the GWR.

How to Find a Station in the Smoke

Clifton Tunnel, Bristol, in the days of steam was very smoky and trains emerging from it into Clifton Down station sometimes overran the platforms because of the murk. To avoid the embarrassment of a driver having to reverse, a clapper and gong were installed near the tunnel mouth to warn drivers that they were nearing the exit.

From Canal to Railway

The Camerton branch just south of Bath is famous for being the location for the film *The Titfield Thunderbolt*. Its route started as the Somerset Coal Canal, but this became redundant. When the railway was planned, it used much of the course of the canal and two features were recycled: a tunnel at Combe Hay and a footbridge at Monkton Combe. Dated at 1800 and 1811 respectively, they were the oldest, or one of the oldest, railway structures in the world.

Steep Inclines Worked by Adhesion

On the North British Railway the goods line to Kirkcaldy Harbour had a gradient of 1 in 20 for 600 yards, while the Oldham incline of the London & North Western Railway was 1 in 27 for approximately three-quarters of a mile, as was the North Pembrokeshire branch of the GWR. The SR's Ilfracombe branch had 2 miles of 1 in 36, whereas the gradient on the Birmingham & Gloucester's Lickey Incline is 1 in 37½.

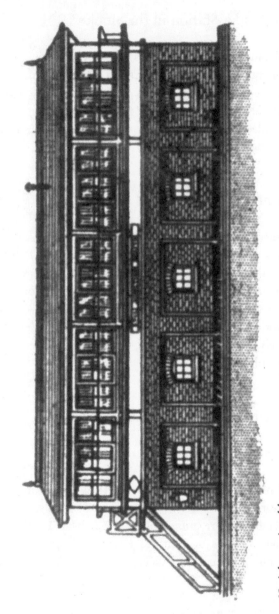

65. A large signal box.

The Largest Signal Boxes

The Glasgow & South Western Railway's station at Glasgow, St Enoch had 488 levers, the next largest being the Caledonian Railway's Glasgow Central with 374. The largest English box was the Loco Yard at York, with 295 levers.

5

Accidents

The Author's Narrow Escape from Death

The author had a narrow escape from being killed by a locomotive toppling over on him.

Like so many boys, I was very keen on railways and spent hours collecting engine numbers. One sunny afternoon in mid-August, feeling replete after a good lunch, I was sitting on the slope of a cutting beside the GWR main line to the West of England.

Before long, a Brunswick green tank engine appeared pulling two tea-and-cream-coloured coaches. For a stopping train it was going quite quickly, I remember estimating its speed at around 60 mph.

I strained my eyes to glimpse the number, because the small brass number plates favoured by the Great Western were not easy to read at speed. As it passed I heard a loud noise and the engine swayed violently. It was passing over some points at the time, so a I assumed that crossing these at speed caused the rocking and dismissed the matter from my mind.

I jotted the number in my notebook and gave the train a cursory glance, expecting to see it disappearing into a tunnel. Much to my surprise it was grinding to a halt only 250 yards away. To add to my amazement, the guard and fireman jumped down and hurried back, the signalman throwing his signals to danger and joining them.

By now I had nervously taken refuge behind the parapet of an overbridge. As they reached near the spot where I had been standing, they bent down and began to pick up pieces of metal and throw them up the side of the cutting. Looking down on the permanent way from the bridge, I noticed that one sleeper had been split in half.

Late that day, having bribed my way into the signal box with the aid of some windfall pears, I was able to learn the full story.

As the engine crossed the points, a spring supporting one of the driving wheels had broken and the signalman from his almost head-on vantage point, thought it was going to overturn. Had it done so, it would have landed at my feet. It was, indeed, a very narrow escape and I was very lucky not to have been killed by flying metal from the broken spring.

A Narrow Escape

On 24 September 1954 a soldier injured himself one night when he fell across the track near Crowthorne on the Guildford to Reading line. Unable to move, he feared being struck by a train. To try and obviate this, he set fire to his tunic as a warning sign. The flames were not seen in time to stop a train striking him a glancing blow which knocked him clear of the track, the only injury being to his hand.

Charles Dickens Is Involved in an Accident

The time of the boat train to Folkestone varied according to the tide. Timetables were issued each month so that stations,

66. A sketch of the Staplehurst disaster on the morning after the crash.

signal boxes and permanent way staff would know when this tidal train could be expected.

Near Staplehurst, a bridge over a small stream called the Beult required its longitudinal sleepers to be replaced. Back in 1865 this job was done between trains and on 9 June only one of the thirty-two baulks still needed replacing.

That day the foreman unfortunately looked up the wrong date and after the previous train had passed, set about replacing the timber. To make matters worse, he posted the lookout man nearer the bridge than the regulations stated.

Soon after the rails had been lifted the train approached at full speed. The warning from the lookout was insufficient to allow the driver to brake in time. At the gap in the rails, the engine crashed down on to the bridge and ploughed along. Fortunately the engine and the first two coaches reached the far side, but the couplings between the second and third carriages snapped. The remaining five coaches crashed into the swampy fields and the River Beult killing ten passengers and injuring forty-nine. Charles Dickens was a passenger and actually reading through the manuscript of *Our Mutual Friend* when the accident occurred.

Although Dickens was not physically hurt, the experience so affected his nervous system that he never really recovered and died, aged fifty-seven on 9 June 1870, exactly five years after the accident.

It Never Rains But It Pours

Railway accidents are fortunately so rare that the chance of two accidents happening at the same location are very slim, however two tragedies occurred at Norton Fitzwarren, just west of Taunton.

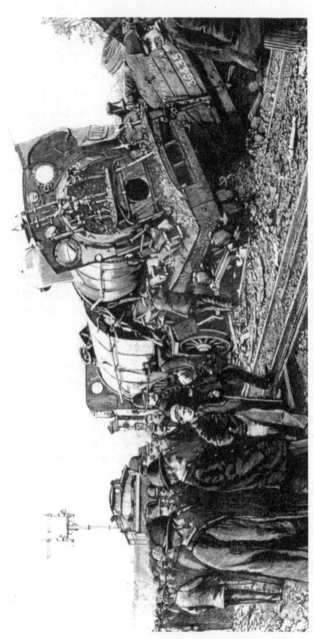

67. Norton Fitzwarren 11 November 1890: broad gauge 4-4-0ST No. 2051 on the left; standard gauge 0-6-0 No. 1100 on the right.

68. Norton Fitzwarren 11 November 1890: broad gauge 4-4-0ST No. 2051 on the left; standard gauge 0-6-0 No. 1100 on the right right.

About 12.30 a.m. on 11 November 1890 a standard gauge Down goods train arrived at Norton Fitzwarren, After carrying out shunting operations, it was shunted to the Up road to allow a fast Down goods train to pass. Unfortunately the signalman forgot about this train standing on the Up road and accepted a fast train conveying passengers from a South African Cape liner from Plymouth to Paddington. The broad gauge engine crashed into the standard gauge engine at 60 mph; the broad gauge engine and coaches remained upright and in line, but ten passengers were killed and nine seriously injured.

On 4 November 1940, breaking with the usual custom, the 9.50 p.m. Paddington to Penzance sleeper was sent from Taunton to Norton Fitzwarren on the Down Relief line. The driver unfortunately failed to realise this in the wartime blackout, mistook the main line signals for his own and the train derailed at the trap points, killing twenty-seven passengers.

The accident could have been even worse, because, as the engine of the express was derailed, a newspaper train was passing on the main line. The guard of the newspaper train did not notice passing the express, but when struck by an object flying through a window, applied his brake and brought the newspaper train to a halt. He found nothing wrong and the train proceeded.

And the object which hit the guard? A rivet head from the bogie frame of the express engine and daylight revealed that the lower panels of the last newspaper van were marked by ballast flung up by the derailed express. Had the newspaper train been just a few seconds later it would have hurtled into the crowded derailed coaches making the fatalities run to three figures.

One Canadian soldier remembers the accident most vividly. He was sitting on the toilet when the accident occurred and was most embarrassed when his actions were exposed to view!

A Riot of Fun

Some accidents can be most amusing, as the accident at Writhlington in 1936 demonstrates. On 29 July 1936 an engine, after shunting, was standing on the main line at Writhlington, near Radstock, Somerset, when the driver was horrified to see a goods train approaching on the same line. He noticed that there was no one on the footplate because the crew had jumped off and were busily pinning down wagon brakes to avoid the impending collision. Swiftly thinking how a collision could be avoided, the shunting engine driver opened the regulator, jumped off his own engine, swung on to the footplate of the runaway and brought it to a halt.

But pride comes before a fall. As he leapt from his side of the cab, his fireman, not hearing his driver's shout telling him to remain on his engine, jumped off the other side, so now no one was on board the shunting engine which was running away propelling eight wagons.

It sped along to Midford where its speed was estimated to be 50 mph. The double track here became single and seven of the wagons were derailed felling signals, telegraph poles and the signal box. Six wagons shot down a 40-foot-high retaining wall into a garden. The owner subsequently managed to secure the wreckage for firewood at a very reasonable figure. The debris fortunately missed a house, the roof of which was several feet below rail level. The stationmaster, hearing the loud crash, lay on the floor of his office.

The shunting engine kept to the rails and careered on her way pushing before her like a coster's barrow, the remains of a wagon running on only two wheels.

Remarkably this curious vehicle succeeded in negotiating a mile-long tunnel, but near the outskirts of Bath the end door of the wagon fell off, derailing the locomotive's rear wheels and bringing it to a halt. About the same time, owing to a shortage of water, the fusible plug on the firebox crown melted and put the fire out.

Overcome by Fumes

The tunnel mentioned above caused several fatalities.

On 20 November 1929 Somerset & Dorset 2-8-0 No. 89, steaming poorly, struggled up the gradient to Combe Down Tunnel and entered it at 4 mph. One thing in Driver Jennings favour was that he was going tender first, so the chimney was behind him and the fumes less likely to be a problem.

Soon after entering the tunnel on a rising gradient of 1 in 100, it proved to be exceptionally hot and smoky. Fireman Pearce was forced by the choking fumes to wrap a coat round his head and sit down, after which he remembered nothing – the gasses had rendered him unconscious.

Jennings gallantly stuck to his post at the regulator, but he too was overcome and fell into unconsciousness. At the post-mortem at least 75 per cent of his blood was saturated with carbon monoxide.

No. 89, now with two insensible men on her footplate, plodded up through the tunnel. The other side was a gradient of 1 in 50 down to Bath. Helped by the weight of thirty-eight vehicles behind her, No. 89 picked up speed. Guard Christopher Wagner applied the handbrake in his van, but without the help of the locomotive and tender brakes it was little more than a gesture.

The train sped round the curve by Bath Junction and, at a probable speed of 50–60 mph, derailed at the second set of points in the goods yard, ran between the tracks for about 50 yards, before striking the shed and overturning, causing wagons to pile up in a great heap, with thirty destroyed or beyond repair.

The near end of the office cabin was demolished killing Inspector John Norman, one curiosity being that a pencil on the office table was driven into a sleeper for about half its length. A railway employee taking a short cut across the yard was killed when struck on the head by part of a gas lamp standard.

Driver Jennings was just alive, but died on his way to hospital. Pearce was alive, but badly injured. Guard Wagner was also seriously hurt. Anticipating a derailment on the curve at Bath Junction, he jumped from his van and on landing received a compound fracture to both legs. Ironically had he stayed in his van he would have been unharmed, for after the crash it still stood upright with his oil lamp burning brightly and with not a milk bottle overturned. This should not have been surprising because the brake was screwed on hard thus keeping the couplings taut, so when the front wagons piled up and the rest stopped, the buffers of the brake van and the wagon before it would not have touched.

A live coal from No. 89 was flung through an open window where it caught a nearby house alight, but fortunately the fire was soon put out.

Newspaper photographers arrived from London by the first train but were denied permits. Determined not to be outwitted, they boarded an outward train from the station which luckily for them came to a stand close by the scene of the accident and thus they were able to obtain their pictures.

Hooked

In March 1900 just as the 7.40 p.m. coal train from Whitstable Harbour to Canterbury was leaving Whitstable, a farm worker, William Atkins, begged from the guard a lift for himself and his bicycle as he had missed the 7.30 p.m. passenger train and did not wish to wait until 9.00 p.m. for the next. The guard agreed and helped Atkins place the bicycle in his van.

In due course the train stopped to set him down near his home and the guard took the opportunity of joining the enginemen on the footplate for the remainder of the journey to Canterbury.

Unfortunately as the train moved away, Atkins stumbled in the dark and caught his belt over the brake van's rear coupling hook.

Dangerously hanging over the track, he managed to hook one of his legs over a buffer, but his shouts for help were unheard until they arrived in Canterbury.

Both driver and guard were fined £4 in addition to being severely reprimanded.

In October 1912 a similar incident occurred one night to Shunter Percy Borwon at Maidstone. He was collecting his shunting pole from across the buffers just as the 'Right Away' was given. In his haste to get clear his foot slipped on a greasy sleeper and he fell against the engine and its front coupling hook caught in his leather belt. His shouts were unheard and he travelled 8 miles in this uncomfortable and frightening manner before a signalman spotted him and stopped the train. As a result the South Eastern Railway issued a circular that warned employees of the dangers of wearing thick belts.

Glasgow Queen Street Accident

Leaving Glasgow Queen Street station, the line climbs through a tunnel on a gradient of 1 in 44. Most trains were provided with a rear-banking engine, but on 12 October 1928 the 9.45 p.m. to Edinburgh was divided and the first portion, weighing only 137 tons, was not provided with assistance. Unfortunately the engine stalled in the tunnel and in attempting to start, the driver inadvertently reversed it. Not realising in the smoky conditions of the tunnel that he was travelling backwards instead of forwards, he collided with a train which, after the departure of the express, had been allowed to follow it from the station into the tunnel in order to set back into another road. Unfortunately four passengers were killed.

Before stalling, the express had cleared the electrical fouling bars which extended 320 yards into the tunnel and the smoke was so thick that the driver could not see the seven electric lights which had been placed on the tunnel wall to assist drivers in verifying the direction of their movement following a similar accident in 1925; they extended to a point well beyond the fouling bars. These lights were automatically illuminated when the Queen Street signalman lowered any of the starting signals giving admission to the tunnel and were switched off by an automatic treadle as the train left the Cowlairs end. There was a rule that no movement into the tunnel was permitted until the switching off of the lights proved that the preceding train had cleared the switching-off treadle. The Ministry of Transport apportioned all the blame for the accident on the Queen Street signalman for having failed to take the necessary precaution.

A Curious Derailment

In the autumn of 1904 a goods train became divided just outside of Truro during the night. When the guard came to recouple the wagons he found he had only thirty-two; two had vanished.

When daylight came, the missing two were found on an embankment standing clear of the main line. In running round the curve they must have continued on a straight course, but the fact that the coupling chains in front and behind the two wagons should have snapped without diverting other vehicles seems incredible.

Another Curious Derailment

On 23 January 1930 Lord Nelson class 4-6-0 No. E853 *Sir Richard Grenville* was working the 4.57 p.m. Dover Marine to Victoria with a load of ten Pullman cars, one four-wheeled luggage van and a six-wheeled luggage van.

Two minutes late and travelling at 50–55 mph between Beckenham Junction (East) and Herne Hill (West), it became derailed at Kent House station. At some crossovers just beyond Kent House, No. E853 managed to get herself back on the track.

The driver said that he only felt a slight roll going through the station and this was usual at that location and, quite unaware of the derailment, reached Victoria 'Right time'.

At the subsequent Ministry of Transport inquiry, it was revealed that a speed restriction of 40 mph was in place at Kent House.

The Sevenoaks Derailment

SR 2-6-4T No. 800 *River Cray* was working the 5.00 p.m. Cannon Street to Folkestone on 24 August 1927. Midway between Dunton Green and Sevenoaks the driver heard a knocking sound and immediately closed the regulator and applied the brake as he believed the leading pair of wheels had left the track.

Unfortunately the derailed wheels met a pair of trailing catch points which were split open and the whole train derailed. This might not have been too serious but for the fact that an

69. A steam-powered breakdown crane with runner wagon on the left.

overbridge with a central pier was beyond and some of the coaches piled against it killing thirteen passengers and seriously injuring twenty-one.

This incident was not the first with this class of engine and all other members of this class of locomotive were ordered to remain on shed until a thorough investigation had been carried out.

These engines were proved to be inherently unstable at high speed on anything less than perfect track: an engine of the class rode satisfactorily when tested on the LNER main line at 83 mph, but rolled severely on SR track. The problem was caused by the Brighton and South Eastern sections of the SR using shingle ballast on ash foundations, while the use of King Arthur class 4-6-0s and heavier coaches had knocked the permanent way about. The line was subsequently improved by being ballasted with Meldon stone and the 2-6-4Ts rebuilt as 4-6-0 tender engines.

A Back to Front Engine

In 1887 the GWR built twenty 0-4-2Ts with double frames. The design of the trailing axle boxes caused dangerous swaying, so were replaced with a bogie having the wooden Mansell wheels normally only seen on passenger coaches. This alteration did not solve the problem and the locomotives were still unsteady, so in 1899 they were turned back to front becoming 4-4-0 tender engines and lived happily ever after.

How to Prevent a Murder

In 1864 Franz Muller murdered Thomas Briggs in a North London Railway train near Old Ford. In order to try and avoid a repetition of such goings-on in a compartment, certain lines, notably the London & South Western Railway, cut port holes in the partitions so that the interior of a compartment could be seen from one adjoining. These windows were known as 'Muller's lights', but were disliked for various amorous reasons, sympathetically delineated in the various pages of *Punch*.

The Board of Trade also insisted that some form of communication should be installed on all trains between passengers, the guard and the driver. The system approved by the Board was a rope running along the outside of the carriages connected to a bell on the engine. It proved very unreliable as you had to pull in a long length of slack on the rope before the bell sounded and in an emergency there was just not the time for this.

6

Narrow Gauge Railways

The Ravensglass & Eskdale Railway

The Ravensglass & Eskdale Railway has had a particularly interesting history. Opened as a 2 foot 9 inch gauge line on 24 May 1875 it closed on 30 November 1908, but reopened for goods in April 1911 and closed in 1913.

This was still not the end of the story for it reopened as a 15 inch gauge line to Muncaster in August 1915, reaching Boot in April 1917. As a stone-crushing plant 2½ miles up the line from Ravensglass supplied granite ballast for the LMS, in order to avoid transfer of the ballast from narrow to standard gauge wagons at Ravensglass, mixed gauge was laid between Murthwaite and Ravensglass. This, unlike the tourist trade, provided a constant all-year-round income. Latterly the standard gauge section was worked by a diesel 0-6-0.

The 3 foot gauge Southwold Railway ran for 8¾ miles from the Great Eastern's Ispwich to Lowestoft line at Halesworth to Southwold. Opened in 1879 it boosted the town's fishing and tourist industry. Unfortunately bus competition caused its closure in 1929.

Instead of being scrapped, the railway was simply abandoned. Vandals were not so prevalent in those days and an enthusiast visiting in July 1939 found that only one of the fifty vehicles

Sec., H. Carne.]		HALESWORTH and SOUTHWOLD.—Southwold.				[Man. Director, A. C. Pain.

Up.

Fares 1 cl. 3 cl.		mrn	mrn	aft	aft	aft	aft	aft	Sundays aft	aft
	Southwold dep	7 30	10 50	12 47	2 50	5 25	7 10		1 40	8 10
20. 1	Walberswick *a*	7 33	10 53	12 50	2 53	5 28	7 13		1 43	8 13
60. 4	Blythburgh * *a*	7 45	11 5	1 2	3 5	5 40	7 25		1 55	8 25
100. 6½	Wenhaston *a*	7 56	11 16	1 13	3 16	5 51	7 36		2 6	8 36
2.0. 9	Haleswrth 13 2	8 7	11 27	1 24	3 27	6 2	7 47		2 17	8 47

Down.

		mrn	non	aft	aft	aft	aft	Sundays aft	aft
	Halesworth dep	8 50	12 01	1 30	3 43	6 13	8 9	2 20	8 50
	Wenhaston *a*	8 59	12 9	1 39	3 52	6 22	8 18	2 29	5 59
	Blythburgh * *a*	9 10	12 20	1 50	4 3	6 33	8 29	2 40	9 10
	Walberswick *a*	9 24	12 34	2 4	4 17	6 47	8 43	2 54	9 24
	Southwold ..arr	9 27	12 37	2 7	4 20	6 50	8 46	2 57	9 27

☞ All 1 & 3 class. **a** Stop by signal to take up, and set down on informing the Guard. * Station for Wangford.

70. The Southwold Railway timetable for August 1887.

had been destroyed by fire and the 2-4-0T No. 3 *Blythe* was still standing in the shed near Halesworth, though bereft of her smaller fittings. Some trees more than 10 feet high grew between some sleepers. At all the stations except Southwold, papers, letters and books were there just as they had been left on the day of closure, only the ticket stocks had been removed. In the engine shed at Southwold were 2-4-0T No. 2 *Halesworth* and 0-6-0T No. 4 *Wenhaston*.

The reason for the railway being left almost untouched was that the Town Clerk of Southwold, who in 1933 had been appointed receiver for the railway because of arrears of rates due to the Southwold Town Council, was unwilling to dispose of any property without the passing of an enabling Act of Parliament.

On 7 June 1940 the Southwold Town Council decided that the attention of the salvage department of the Ministry of Supply be drawn to the derelict rolling stock and requested the department to exercise the rights conferred upon it by the Emergency Powers Act in order to obtain the stock for conversion into munitions. The Halesworth Urban District Council had previously passed a similar resolution.

Practise What You Preach

When the 1-foot-11½-inch gauge Lynton & Barnstaple Railway was threatened with closure, a protest meeting was held at Barnstaple. On inquiry, most of the protesters had arrived by road!

7

Light Railways

Arthur Pain, trained by R. P. Brereton, I. K. Brunel's chief assistant, envisaged a scheme for light railways providing transport in districts which could not economically be served by conventional railways. He believed the answer to be a combination of a railway and tramway with minimal earthworks and thus have a low cost of construction. Instead of stations with platforms and buildings, expense could be kept down by simply picking up passengers where a line met a road at a level crossing. Signalling would be minimal, while the cost of maintaining a crossing keeper could be avoided by whistling and slowing trains over a crossing to 5 mph, and animals being prevented from wandering along the line by installing cattle grids – sloping lengths of timber slats looking very much like an organ pedal-board and almost impossible to walk on.

Two Acts of Parliament favoured Pain's proposal. The Railway Construction Facilities Act of 1864 permitted a railway to be built without the need for an Act as long as all landowners on the route agreed to sell the land required by the railway company. This facility avoided the considerable legal expenses in obtaining an Act.

The Regulation of Railways Act, passed four years later in 1868, enabled a light railway to be constructed under conditions laid down by the Board of Trade. A 'light railway' – the term first appeared in the 1868 Act – was generally defined as a line allowing a maximum weight of eight tons per axle and a speed limit of 25 mph. Pain believed that landowners would support such a scheme due to the increased value it would bring to their property and trade. The first light railway in England was the Culm Valley Light Railway in Devon which opened 29 May 1876.

Interestingly, the Bideford, Westward Ho! Appledore Railway in North Devon had several curiosities, not least the fact that it had an exclamation mark in its title and was probably the only railway in the world to have this feature. It was there because the settlement of Westward Ho! took its name from Charles Kingsley's novel.

While the line was still under construction the concern was taken over by British Electric Traction, a company whose principal interest was in electrically-powered street tramways. The line never used electric propulsion but owned three 2-4-2T steam locomotives, not quite conventional as they were fitted

71. A Bideford, Westward Ho! & Appledore Railway excursion ticket.

with side plates to conceal wheels and motion. This was laid down by law for all steam locomotives which worked on public streets, the street in this instance being Bideford Quay. When travelling on this section the fireman stood at the front of the engine ringing the warning bell.

The line opened to the public on 18 May 1901. A strange clause in the timetable read:

> The published timetables are only intended to fix the time before which the trains will not start, and the company do not undertake that the trains shall start or arrive at the times specified in the tables.

The passenger coaches, lit by acetylene gas, were of the American pattern with end balconies and steps giving access to and from the station platforms which were only six inches or a foot in height. These vehicles were unusual in having a single central buffer – common on the narrow gauge, but probably unique on British standard gauge. Another unconventional feature was that some coaches had double-faced clocks displayed inside.

Another peculiarity was that next to Westward Ho! station the railway built Station Hall for concerts, with combined rail and admission tickets being issued. This hall also doubled as an extra waiting room in inclement weather, or as an extra office, or storage room.

During the First World War the government commandeered locomotives and track from various railways to take to France to assist with transport to and from the front lines. The Bideford & Westward Ho! Railway was one of those selected and was completely closed on 28 March 1917. As it was not connected with any other line, the three locomotives were removed by temporary track being laid over Bideford Bridge to give access to the London & South Western Railway.

One fascinating light railway in the 'grey' area between a street tramway and an ordinary railway was the Wisbech & Upwell Tramway owned by the Great Eastern Railway. It passed through a rich fruit-growing district close to the boundary of Norfolk and the Isle of Ely. The line, opened to Wisbech in 1884, was economically constructed, costing only £2,284 per mile, compared with the £12,000 per mile of a typical branch line.

As it was laid in part alongside a public road, strict regulations were laid down by the Board of Trade. Locomotives were required to be fitted with a governor, with which the driver could not tamper, to shut off steam and apply the brakes if a speed of 10 mph was exceeded. The overall speed limit was 8 mph and 4 mph when passing over points. Offences were punished by a fine of £10. Engines were required to carry a warning bell and a fender to push aside any obstruction. Blast from the chimney had to be noiseless and the machinery free from audible clatter. The locomotive's motion was enclosed by a skirt reaching to within four inches of the ground. The entrance and exit from the carriages had to be by the rear platform of the tramcar-type coaches with end platforms and gangways. Trains stopped to pick up or set down passengers anywhere along the line.

The single track line joined the GER's King's Lynn to March line just west of Wisbech passenger station, the tramway engines working along the main line to the goods depot. Wisbech station had a side platform with a height suitable for the low-built tramcars. With the rise of motor transport, and the severe speed limit imposed on the tramway, the passenger service was withdrawn on 2 January 1928.

Heavy goods traffic continued, fruit being the most important and during the strawberry, plum and apple seasons the sidings were often filled to capacity with fruit vans. In 1937 three freight trains ran daily. The terminus at Upwell was extensive with seven long sidings, with loading spaces between them and a cattle dock, while the passenger station had a terminal road and run-round loop.

Gates were provided at places where the tramway left or entered its own right of way but, except at Wisbech, they were disused. Apart from signals at the junction with the main line and a starting signal at Wisbech, there were no other signals, train movements being controlled by telephone.

The GER built two classes of tram engines for use on the Wisbech tramway, a 0-4-0T and 0-6-0T, and also for use on the quayside lines at Ipswich, Lowestoft and Yarmouth. In order that the driver could have a good view ahead, the controls were duplicated at each end. To make them quieter, a driver could operate a lever diverting the exhaust into the water tanks, while steam from the safety valves was also directed there.

In 1930 the LNER purchased two Sentinel four-wheeled, geared, 200 hp double cab locomotives with the engine unit in one cab and the boiler in the other, the water tank situated between the two. In later years diesel traction was used, but the line eventually closed on 23 May 1966.

Britain's First Passenger-Carrying Railway

The Swansea & Mumbles Railway began as a horse-worked, freight-only line in 1806. The following year saw a contract for the right to run 'a waggon or wagons ... for the conveyance of passengers'. This, on 25 March 1807, was the earliest known record of the regular carrying by rail of passengers anywhere in the world. Benjamin French paid the company £20 a year in lieu of tolls.

The earliest reference in a published work to the line appeared in 1809 when Miss Elizabeth Isabella Spence issued her *Summer Excursions through Parts of Oxfordshire, Gloucestershire,*

MAY, 1869.

SWANSEA AND MUMBLES.

Oystermouth Railway Time Table.

For Conveyance of Goods, Hire of **SPECIAL CARRIAGES**, and **SALE OF TICKETS**, at a **DISCOUNT**, apply to Mr. R. WILLIAM, at the Station, Rutland Street, Swansea.

NOTICE.—To **TOURISTS** and **VISITORS**.—The **MUMBLES** is replete with every accommodation for Visitors, picturesquely situated in the immediate vicinity of lofty rocks, the extensive Ruins of Oystermouth Castle, and the Bays of Langland, Bracelet, and Caswell, renowned for their bathing sands, rare shells, and sea flowers.

☞ **TIME TABLES** may be had of Mr. HERBERT JONES, Printer, 81, Oxford Street, Swansea.

N.B.—Passengers will not be entitled to claim for the loss of, or damage done to, any Luggage while on the Carriages or Premises of this Line, unless the same has been booked and paid for, the value not to exceed Ten Shillings.

Season Tickets will be issued on and after the 1st March, 1869, apply at the Swansea Station.

Additional Trains will run on WHIT MONDAY.

72. The Oystermouth Railway timetable for May 1869.

73. The two-legged horse in the sketch of a coach used on the Oystermouth Railway painted by J. Ashford in 1819.

Warwickshire, Staffordshire, Herefordshire, Derbyshire and South Wales. She wrote:

> I never spent an afternoon with more delight than the former one in exploring the romantic scenery of Oystermouth. I was conveyed there in a carriage of a singular construction, built for the conveniency of parties, who go hence to Oystermouth to spend the day. This car contains twelve persons and is constructed chiefly of iron, its four wheels run on an iron railway by the aid of one horse, and is an easy and light vehicle.

The original permanent way consisted of 3-foot-lengths of angle iron fastened to granite blocks by dog spikes, the vehicle wheels being flangeless.

By 1855 the passenger service had become redundant due to a bus service running along a new parallel road. That year part of the line was re-laid with edge rails to carry coal to Swansea and in 1860 a horse-drawn passenger service was revived. The Swansea Improvements & Tramways Company introduced steam locomotives in 1877, though some trains continued to use horse haulage. Horse traction ended in 1896 when a small tank engine drew enormous double-decker open-top tramcars along the line. In 1902–03 an experiment was made with battery-electric tramcars. In 1929 large double-decker electric trams appeared, each seating 109 passengers. In 1945 five million passengers were carried, but following this, as road competition numbers declined, the railway closed in 1960.

The line had been famous for its two-legged horse. The animal really had the conventional four legs, but a sketch painted by J. Ashford in 1819 only showed two.

Mountain Railways

Britain has two mountain railways: one climbing Snaefell and the other Snowdon.

The Snaefell Mountain Railway opened in 1895 using single-decker electric tramcars powered from an overhead line. It climbs 1,823 feet in 4½ miles mainly at 1 in 12. Unlike the 3 foot gauge of its owners, the Manx Railway, the 3 foot 6 inch gauge was chosen to enable the Manx Northern Railway steam locomotives to be used during construction.

Today, cars are fitted with both an electric regenerative braking system and the Fell brake, where pairs of horizontal wheels grip a centre rail.

The 2 foot 7½ inch gauge was opened by Snowdon Mountain Railway on 6 April 1896, but was immediately closed due to track defects. Extensive alterations and repairs were effected and the line reopened on 19 April 1897. It climbs 3,140 feet in 4½ miles on a ruling gradient of 1 in 5½.

The 0-4-2T locomotives built by the Swiss Locomotive Works were of two types, those built in 1895–96 have long side tanks and the drive from the cylinders to the wheels is transmitted by a large oscillating lever in the front of the engine. As the fulcrum of this lever is at the bottom end and the drive from the cylinders at its top end, this imparts a surging motion both when climbing and when descending using the counter-pressure brake.

The newer engines, built in 1923, have short tanks and the drive is altered by arranging the fulcrum of the oscillating lever at its centre, thus ensuring a more even torque. The earlier engines were saturated whereas those of 1923 were superheated and used two hundredweights of coal less on each journey.

On the flat, the boiler tips forward in order to maintain a horizontal water level when climbing. In order to climb without slipping, the Abt system is used whereby a pair of co-axial pinions engages in staggered teeth on the central double-rack rail.

Both engines and coaches are fitted with a centrifugal governor set to give a maximum speed of 5 mph in each direction and should this speed be exceeded, a trip gear operates and fully applies all of the brakes. The coach is not coupled to the engine, but rests against a central buffer, the gradient keeping the two units together. The coaches are additionally fitted with a powerful handbrake operated by the conductor.

Getting the Bride to Church

On 23 December 1933 the daughter of a Dungeness fisherman was to be married at Lydd church and rail was the only reasonable way of crossing 2 miles of shingle in a wedding dress. Although the Romney, Hythe & Dymchurch Light Railway was not normally open during the winter, its owner, Captain Howie, graciously organised a special train for her.

The Grimsby & Immingham Electric Railway

The Grimsby & Immingham line was particularly interesting as it was an amalgam of a railway and tramway.

Constructed under the Grimsby Light Railways Order of 1906 it opened in May 1912 and with the completion of the Great Central Railway's Immingham docks, the line was extended to a new terminus in November 1912. Primarily intended for the conveyance of dock workmen, the railway maintained a day and night service. For 4½ miles the electric line ran parallel with the railway tracks to the docks, but then joined a road.

More cars were required to supplement the original GCR vehicles and in 1948 BR purchased three bogie single-deckers from Newcastle-on-Tyne Corporation, though they were disliked at their new home. In about 1951 nineteen single-deckers were obtained from Gateshead & District Tramways Company. Only eighteen cars were actually required, but one was damaged beyond repair while being unloaded and the nineteenth bought as a replacement. The original Great Central Railway cars bore a notice earnestly requesting passengers to refrain from spitting. Another curiosity was a notice exhibited in the tramways shelter at Immingham Dock giving details of services and fares in seven languages: English, Dutch, German, Italian, Norwegian, Spanish and Swedish. Not far from the terminus were British Railways' Immingham Dock Refreshment & Dining Rooms divided into first, second and third class accommodation.

The Weston, Clevedon & Portishead Light Railway

The WC&P was a typical light railway, offering a figure of fun, not least because of the amusement one could have with its initials! It was the kind of line where trains sometimes stopped for passengers to get out and pick mushrooms or blackberries. It was run on a shoe string and because traffic was heavier in the summer than in the winter, in the latter season some staff were employed making concrete sleepers – it being one of the first railways in Britain to use them. It was an early user of internal combustion engines in its vehicles, purchasing a Drewry railcar as early as 1921 and the same year a Muir-Hill rail-tractor was purchased, consisting of a Fordson tractor fitted with flanged wheels. Unfortunately when being towed behind a train it became derailed and before the train could be stopped was smashed to pieces.

o Bridge

Wick St Lawrence Church 'n Cross

terior of Carriage

tation at Clevedon

74. Sketches of the original carriages of the Weston, Clevedon & Portishead Railway.

WESTON, CLEVEDON & PORTISHEAD RAILWAY.

FIRST CLASS FREE PASS No. 3

Expiring unless previously recalled *31st December* 1936

Pass *Dr. & Mrs Macleod*

between *All Stations*

NOT TRANSFERABLE.

Signature
of Holder

The holder of this Pass may also be required to give a specimen signature.

This Pass must be produced for examination when called for by the Officers of the Company, and upon the day of expiry must be returned to General Manager's Office, Tonbridge, Kent.

The Holder is subject to the same Rules and Regulations as other Passengers.

This Pass is granted upon the understanding that it is to be taken as evidence of an agreement that the Company over whose lines it is available are not to be held liable for any pecuniary or other responsibility to the Holder for loss of life, personal injury or delay, or for loss of or delay or damage to property however caused, that may be sustained by such person while using the Pass. W. H. AUSTEN,
                                            General Manager.

Issued by

75. Weston, Clevedon & Portishead Railway first class free pass issued 31 December 1936 to the company's doctor and his wife.

8

Railways & Royalty

Four private stations were provided solely for royalty: Nine Elms, London; Gosport Dockyard, used when Queen Victoria travelled to and from the Isle of Wight; Whippingham, the station for Osborne; and St Margaret's, Edinburgh.

Several stations had royal waiting rooms. The first GWR station at Windsor was simply a standard GWR train shed distinguished by a row of windows above the pediment to raise the roof level.

In 1882 an attempt was made to shoot Queen Victoria as her carriage left Windsor station. Fortunately the assassination attempt was unsuccessful.

Lacking sufficient space for royal occasions, the GWR provided a much more spacious affair at Windsor as a Diamond Jubilee present. A special royal station was erected a road-width away from the new public station, with a covered entrance spanning the driveway separating the two. The entrance arch of brick and stone carried the GWR coat of arms and the windscreen below had the words 'Great Western Railway' in ornate brass lettering. The wide platform at the royal station was spanned by a glazed train shed, 'To keep my soldiers dry', as requested by the queen. The platform was spacious enough to turn the royal carriage and accommodate a full military escort, either mounted or on foot.

76. The attempt to shoot Queen Victoria outside Windsor station, 2 March 1882.

77. Windsor Castle *c.* 1852 with the GWR terminus on the far right.

SCALE ELEVATION OF THE GREAT WESTERN RAILWAY'S NEW ROYAL TRAIN

SCALE GROUND PLAN OF THE GREAT WESTERN RAILWAY'S NEW ROYAL TRAIN

78. The GWR's new royal train in 1897.

Within the train shed was the royal waiting room, built in the standard GWR style of the period but faced with stone instead of brick. It had a wood-panelled dado and was lit by an art nouveau dome. First used on 21 June 1897 this royal waiting room only contained ladies' accommodation, so following the accession of King Edward VII, it was enlarged in 1902 to provide facilities for gentlemen.

One of the most remarkable runs was made by the train which conveyed the body of Queen Victoria on her last journey from Osborne, Isle of Wight, where she died on 22 January 1901, to Victoria. Because of the number of crowned heads conveyed in the train from Gosport to Victoria, the authorities decided that no photographers should be allowed access to any part of the line, which was patrolled by platelayers, porters and railway officials for its whole length.

The London, Brighton & South Coast Railway's Royal train was used for conveying the body to London. It had travelled to Portsmouth on 23 January carrying Edward VII on his way to participate in the funeral arrangements. It returned empty to Brighton and on 28 January ran back to Portsmouth for test purposes, making an experimental run on the Portsmouth Dockyard south jetty line to test clearances, curves and so forth.

As there was a certain acrimony between the Brighton company and the London & South Western Railway, as both companies served the area, the actual itinerary of the train was not determined until late on 31 January after King Edward VII had personally selected the route and settled outstanding points of difference. He selected the LBSCR route which was interesting as Queen Victoria had an antipathy to that railway – it was rumoured because the title included the name 'Brighton', a place where she had been treated discourteously in the early years of her reign.

The coffin was carried on a bier draped in purple in the centre of a GWR bogie saloon, which the queen had used for many years of travelling. The only light came from the gas lamps fixed in the clerestory roof. The funeral train ran from Clarence Yard, Gosport carrying the coffin, the German emperor and other royal princes via Fareham, Cosham, Havant, Horsham and Dorking to Victoria, the latter station being closed to the public between 9.00 a.m. and 11.00 a.m., advertisements and placards being removed and parts of the old structure cleaned and freshened. LSWR engines and guards were provided from Gosport to Fareham and LBSCR engines and guards beyond.

Unlike the careful arrangements made for the queen's travel when she was alive, her funeral train arrangements were chaotic. A plan of the train had been prepared for guiding the guests, but this had been made out for when it arrived at Victoria and someone had overlooked the fact that the train would need to reverse at Fareham. As a result at Clarence Yard everything was found back to front. The eight-coach train was too long for the short platform so the imperial and royal mourners had to scuttle from one end of the train to the other.

This to-do caused much delay and the LSWR and LBSCR officers were not slow at blaming each other for the deficiency. Departure from Gosport was eight minutes late, while a further two minutes were lost at Fareham. The queen disliked high speeds and stipulated a maximum of 40 mph during daylight and 30 mph at night. As King Edward abhorred unpunctuality, the LBSCR obliged by making a very fast run to Victoria, making up the ten minutes lost time and actually arriving two minutes early, having conveying the dead queen at approximately twice the speed she had ever travelled in her lifetime.

From Victoria the coffin was conveyed on a gun carriage through London to Paddington station where the funeral train was the one which had been used on the occasion of her Diamond

Jubilee in 1897. The same saloon was used to carry the coffin, as on arrival at Victoria it had been taken via Battersea, Addison Road, Uxbridge Road and Westbourne Park to Paddington to be included in the GWR royal funeral train. The whole line from Paddington to Windsor was guarded by picked men drawn from all ranks of the service, who were stationed at 25 yard intervals so that all were within sight and hearing distance of one another.

On arrival at Windsor the hawsers provided to haul the gun carriage were frozen up, so communication cords had to be taken from berthed GWR coaches to provide the necessary means of haulage by seamen.

The End of London & North Western Railway Coach Livery

After preserving its LNWR chocolate and white livery for seventeen years following the grouping of the railways in 1923, which caused the LNWR to become part of the LMS, in 1940 the LMS royal train was painted in the standard LMS red livery. The only vehicle on the LMS still wearing the LNWR livery was the Duke of Sutherland's private saloon. (See page 219).

Queen Mary's Doll's House

Queen Mary's doll's house was exhibited in the Palace of Arts at the 1924 Wembley Exhibition. The LMS directors presented Her Majesty with a miniature facsimile of the company's timetable for the doll's house library.

The miniature timetable measured 1 inch by $\frac{7}{12}$ inch and had been reduced in exact proportions from its original size of 11½ inches by 7½ inches. It could be covered by a halfpenny.

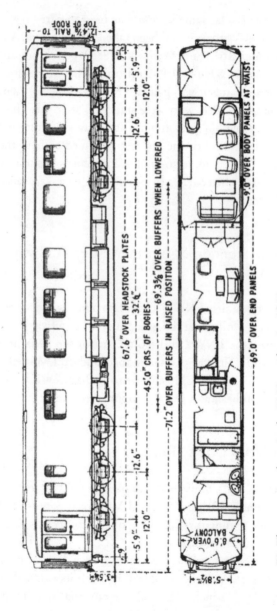

79. The queen's saloon in the LMS royal train, 1941.

Accompanying it was a miniature copy of the *Loch, Mountain and Sea* guide. This was even smaller than the timetable and could be covered by a sixpence, yet the letterpress and illustrations in the guide could be clearly seen with the aid of a magnifying glass.

Writing to the company in acknowledgement of the gift, Her Majesty wrote:

> It is with the greatest pleasure that I say 'thank you' to all the very kind people who have helped to make the Doll's House the most perfect present that anyone could receive, and I hope through showing it at the British Empire Exhibition that it will be the means of raising funds for the many charitable schemes that I have at heart.
> (Signed) Mary R.

Royal Train to Swindon Refreshment Rooms

In around 1900 Swindon Refreshment rooms, known as the Queen's Royal Hotel, were renowned for their splendid catering. Occasionally, the Prince of Wales, (later King Edward VII) even sometimes hired a special train to take his friends there to dinner.

9

Rolling Stock

The Pullman cars on Midland Railway in 1874 comprised the first British train with communication between coaches, but this was via open platforms at the ends of each coach. The first British corridor train was constructed at Swindon in 1891. Communication was by central gangway in the smoking saloons, but by side corridor elsewhere. As far as the passengers were concerned, the corridors led only to the lavatories as the concertina gangways were kept locked, with only the guard having the key. John Pendleton remarked in *Our Railways* that this was 'lest the third class traveller should take a walking tour into the first class carriage, and recline on its morocco and broadcloth, forgetful of the fact that he had not paid the first class fare.'

The gangways were not fitted centrally at the ends of the coaches, but were at one side after the style of Royal Mail van practice. This was no detriment at the time because the train was a set unit, but as the use of corridor trains was extended, the original vehicles had to be converted in order to facilitate coupling-up with later stock with central corridor connections.

The first corridor train with gangway throughout and heated by steam made its appearance on 7 March 1892 between Paddington and Birkenhead. *The Times* of the following day attributed the initiative to the GWR, calling the new service a 'corridor train'.

80. The interior of a Pullman car: notice the spacious one-each-side seating.

In 1896 the GWR was the first British company to attach a restaurant car to a corridor train. The 10.00 a.m. Cardiff to Paddington was described as a 'Through Corridor Luncheon Car Express' but the restaurant car was for the use of first class passengers only. It is interesting to speculate whether the word 'through' refers to the passage through the train, or the fact that it ran through from Paddington to Cardiff, or both.

The Stratford-upon-Avon and Midland Junction Railway was certainly in the forefront of technology. One of its predecessors, the East and West Junction Railway had introduced electric lighting in its coaches around 1900 and by 1910 all were lit by electricity – more than could be said for the larger railway companies. Then in July 1912 a radio message was transmitted from a train between Ettington and Stratford:

> Representatives of railway companies, universities and scientific bodies are today inspecting the von Kramer wireless inductive railophone system for signalling to and from trains to stations. With this system it is possible to stop trains in motion by pressing a button in a signal box. This telegram was dispatched wirelessly from a moving train by the inventor.

Corridor coaches had bars across the windows to steady a passenger walking along a corridor when the riding was rough. Originally of brass, later ones were wood so that they could be easily broken if a coach overturned and passengers needed to escape via the window.

A Railway Prize

Train ferries enabled foreign rolling stock to be brought to British railways and not all of them were returned to their home countries at the start of the Second World War. In 1940 a four-wheeled German wagon was seen in a Down goods train on the Great Central section of the LNER. It was easily recognised by its lengthy wheelbase and by the end guard's compartment in a raised position projecting above one corner of the van. The vehicle carried the inscription 'Deutsche Reichbahn' and 'Saarbrucken', its home town.

Long Trains in the Second World War

Trains of twenty coaches or more were often seen on the LNER main line between London and Scotland during the Second World War. For example, on 31 March 1940 the 10.45 a.m. from Newcastle was made up to twenty-six vehicles from Peterborough to King's Cross, weighing about 762 tons tare, or 850 tons gross. 1,300 passengers were aboard. Worked by a V2 class 2-6-2 it lost only nine minutes on the ninety-three minute schedule.

On 5 April 1940 No. 2509 *Silver Link*, headed the 1.00 p.m. from King's Cross made up of twenty-five vehicles. This was nine coaches longer than the platform and as the first coach was actually in Gasworks Tunnel, special measures were taken to give the driver the 'Right away'.

GWR trains between Paddington and Bristol were limited to sixteen coaches because the platform at Bath station could only hold eight coaches and this involved drawing up twice. Had the trains been any lengthier, they would have had to draw up three times.

Due to a fairly severe curve, the driver of a long Down train was unable to see his guard give the 'Right away'. To overcome this problem, in February 1947 two illuminated indicators were provided, one 20 yards and the other 172 yards in advance of the Down starting signal. Having received intimation from the platform inspector that the train could proceed, the guard operated one of the two push buttons located in boxes on the veranda pillars. This action illuminated the letters 'RA' (Right away). The indicator situated 20 yards in advance of the Down starter showed only in the Bristol direction, but the indicator 172 yards in advance showed in both directions, so was visible to a driver whether his engine was in advance of or to the rear of, the indicator. The indicator was automatically cancelled when the track circuit, to the rear of the Down advanced starting signal became clear.

The fact of trains being too long for the Bath platform almost caused a fatality during the Second World War. A long train came to a stop and a serviceman, assuming his coach was at the platform, in the blackout stepped on to what he believed was the platform, but it was actually a bridge girder. He continued walking and fell into the river. Fortunately he was not drowned, but the GWR fearing a repetition with a fatal ending, erected a fence above the girder.

There were several stations into which the passenger rolling stock of all British main line railways worked daily, Bournemouth West and Newcastle-on-Tyne being two examples. Complete trains of GWR, LNER and SR coaches with their own locomotives could be seen at the GWR station at Oxford, while LMS locomotives and coaches could be seen in the LMS station alongside that of the GWR. Freight trains and locomotives from the GWR, LMS and LNER could be seen at Clapham Junction and also in the SR marshalling sidings at Hither Green.

The Duke of Sutherland was the only owner of a private railway carriage in the British Isles. In 1883 his vast estates were second only to the crown. The most valuable were in Shropshire and Staffordshire, but the greatest acreage was north of Inverness. The railway through Sutherland from Golspie to

Helmsdale was built at the duke's expense. A private station was built at Golspie to serve Dunrobin Castle, the seat of the duke. His line was worked by the Highland Railway, but not sold to that company until 1884.

To enable his railway to be opened before the connection with the Sutherland Railway at Golspie was completed, he purchased a 2-4-0T locomotive and coaches. After the Highland Railway took over, the engine was used to haul the duke's private saloon between Inverness and Dunrobin, but south of Inverness his saloon was attached to main line trains.

In 1892 his son, the fourth duke, decided to have a more powerful engine and this 0-4-4T was designed by David Jones, locomotive superintendent of the Highland Railway. Like its predecessor it was painted dark green with black bands and yellow lining. An unusual feature was a seat with leather cushions extending the full width of the cab provided for passengers riding on the footplate. During the Second World War it performed shunting duties at Invergordon and Rosyth.

In 1899 C. A. Park, the LNWR carriage and wagon superintendent, designed a bogie carriage for the duke. It was a prototype for the royal train built in 1903 for King Edward VII and Queen Alexandra. This train was subsequently used by King George V and Queen Mary, and King George VI and Queen Elizabeth.

With the nationalisation of the railways, the agreement between the Duke of Sutherland and the LMS, whereby he had running powers for his rolling stock over that company's lines, ceased. In February 1949 he advertised his saloon for conversion into a bungalow, but the Lincolnshire Trailer Company purchased it, together with the locomotive and smaller four-wheeled saloon for preservation, In due course it was exhibited on the Romney, Hythe & Dymchurch Railway.

Travelling in a Padded Cell

The first London underground railways were built by the 'cut-and-cover' method whereby a long, deep, wide trench was cut in a street, track laid in the bottom and then roofed. This allowed for a certain amount of ventilation for steam traction, but its construction caused chaos to road users.

A rather less troublesome method was a tube railway laid at a deeper level. As frequent ventilation was impossible, a smoke-free method of propulsion was required. When the City & South London Railway, the first deep-level system in the capital was mooted, it was intended to use cable-haulage which had been successfully used in San Francisco in 1873. To avoid payment of easement fees to landowners, the tubes followed the streets above – this explains why some tubes have sharp curves.

Contracts had been placed for cable-haulage equipment when the directors had second thoughts. The electrically powered Bessbrook & Newry line had been opened in Ireland in 1885, so the City & South London directors placed an order for four-wheel electric locomotives and other equipment.

To fit the 10-foot-6-inch-diameter tunnels, the coaches were only 6 feet 10 inches wide and as there was no scenery to observe, and a conductor called out the names of the stations and opened the trellis gates at the ends of the cars, proper windows were deemed quite unnecessary and only very narrow top lights were provided. As these coaches were heavily stuffed inside, it was inevitable that the public would name them 'padded cells'. The standard gauge was used, though the dimensions of the rolling stock suggested a much narrower gauge.

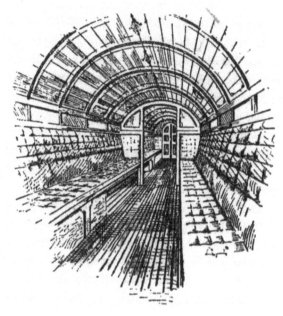

81. The interior of a 'padded cell' on the City & South London Railway.

Railways and the Evacuation of Dunkirk

Railways played a vital part in the evacuation of Dunkirk. Between 20 May and 27 May 1940, fifty-five special troop trains were run from the south-eastern ports as part of the evacuation scheme. However, at 5.00 p.m. on 26 May the SR received instructions for its main scheme, which then began at dawn on 27 May. The first train left the coast at 7.00 a.m. and at 4.00 p.m. on 4 June the scheme ceased to operate. No working notices were issued and the movement was directed by telephone. Matters were made even more difficult for the railways because when some of these trains left the south-east ports, their destinations were unknown but were settled by the military authorities by the time the trains reached key junctions.

It was decided to avoid London as far as possible and therefore cross-country routes had to be worked out at short notice. In some cases this necessitated a slight disturbance to normal passenger services, some of which had to be cancelled or diverted. It was necessary in a few instances to turn over for exclusive military traffic whole sections of line and stations, but alternative road transport facilities were arranged for ordinary traffic.

The extent of the intensity of the operation is indicated by this table:

Date	Number of Trains	Total No. of Officers and Men
20 – (early morning) 27 May	55	24,108
27 May	7	3,386
28 May	31	14,054
29 May	76	38,479
30 May	88	44,938
31 May	107	56,282
1 June	110	59,147
2 June	45	25,123
3 June	51	27,344
4 June	50	26,195
	620	319,056

The outdoor traffic and locomotive staffs in particular were engaged literally night and day, snatching a few hours sleep as the opportunity offered, until the task was completed. The operating difficulties of this military movement were further intensified by the fact that on Sunday 2 June 1940 almost 48,000 children in 70 trains from Kentish and other east-coast towns were evacuated to what were considered safer areas, thirty-two of these trains originating on the SR. Also during the period of the

British Expeditionary Force evacuation British railways carried some 20 million passengers and over 6 million tons of freight.

About the same time as the Dunkirk evacuation, the Ministry of Home Security defined certain districts of the country as defence areas into which movement was restricted. Persons wishing to enter these specified areas for business purposes were not prevented from doing so, but holiday and pleasure visits were banned. Later, these areas were subject to considerable extension and roughly comprised a strip varying in width from Berwick-on-Tweed to Weymouth.

What Happens to Old Railway Coaches?

What happens to old railway coaches? About the year 1900 lots of people had bright ideas for getting further use out of carriages which were no longer fit to run on rails.

One use of an old coach was the 'Hallatrow Mission Carriage' in Somerset. Formerly it had been a GWR flat-sided coach built in 1871 and condemned in 1894 after running for twenty-three years. Its inside dimensions were: 24 feet 6 inches long, 7 feet wide and 6 feet 9 inches high. Inside was a reading desk, a harmonium and rows of seats, four to each row.

The London & South Western Railway Cricket Club naturally used an old coach as its pavilion. One particularly smart alec bought on old London, Brighton & South Coast Railway coach, dumped it in a court at Walworth and lived in it rate free. The local council's lawyers then set to work and the case was brought to a different kind of court. A hard-hearted magistrate ruled the by-law requirements of cubic space to 'live in as a habitual tenement' had been contravened and the owner was ordered to remove it. He refused to budge, but changed his mind when two constables appeared.

At Shoreham bungalows were created from old railway carriages and by 1904 there were about 150 of these. People bought two or three coaches, took off the sides and made a new front and back from new boards, or used more coaches. A wide roof was then put on, often incorporating a veranda. Other coaches were used as summer houses in gardens.

Some children in Scotland had the thrill of being taught in a railway coach. This happened at Gorton, situated in the bleak heart of Rannoch Moor in the Western Highlands.

Gorton had a platform, but was not designated a station and so did not appear in public timetables. Until 1938 the railway employees' children residing in the vicinity were educated at Rannoch, 7 miles away, but the school there proved to be too small to accommodate the Gorton children as well as those in the neighbourhood, so consequently the Argyllshire Education Authority asked the railway company for permission to erect a temporary school on the platform at Gorton and asked whether it would be possible for them to provide a railway carriage for the purpose. This was done and the new school opened in March 1938 attended by eight children. The teacher travelled the 8½ miles from Bridge of Orchy by an express which made a special stop at Gorton.

When the SR electrified part of its South Eastern & Chatham section, the motor coaches were made from the bodies of either one and a half six-wheel, or two four-wheel coaches spliced together and mounted on a new underframe, the driving end being new. To form trailer coaches, the bodies of two four-wheel or six-wheel coaches were mounted on a new underframe, one at each end, the intermediate space being filled by the requisite number of new compartments. Some of the coaches given a new lease of life were already thirty years old.

What Americans Carry in England

An 'American Traveller' wrote to the *Derby Mercury* in July 1854:

> I am not a timid man, but I never enter an English railway carriage without having in my pocket a loaded revolver. How am I to know but that my travelling companion may be a madman escaped from confinement, or a runaway criminal? And what protection have I against their assault if it should please them to attack me, but the weapon I carry?

He went on to suggest communication cords through each compartment, already in use in the United States.

Although the risk of being shot in a British railway carriage is low, there have been some instances of this occurring.

The First Gloucestershire Rifle Volunteer Corps had a range at Avonmouth, also used by Clifton College volunteers. Unfortunately on 16 February 1878 a sixth former, returning on the Clifton Extension Railway from practice, accidentally discharged his rifle, the shot killing a master in the compartment.

Eleven years later, on 7 June 1889, a murder was attempted on a Reading to Trowbridge train. Shortly after leaving Devizes, a platelayer was horrified to see a woman stand and suddenly throw up both arms. A man in the compartment with her fired two shots from a revolver and pushed her out of the carriage window. She then fell on the embankment and was carried by the platelayer and another man to Devizes Cottage Hospital.

Shortly after, a man's mangled corpse was found a quarter of a mile beyond the scene of the first incident. Apparently the man, head over heels in love with the lady, had been rejected as her suitor, perhaps understandably, for he had a history of mental instability. It was believed that he fell under the train when jumping off to escape capture.

Communication Cords

Communication cords are fascinating. Oh how tempting it is to pull that little red chain, or on modern trains, move that red lever, but no, we dare not do it.

My favourite story connected with this subject concerns G. K. Chesterton. A friend once remarked to the writer: 'I'd gladly give £10 if we could stop the train here for five minutes – that's the finest view in Europe.' G. K. stood up. 'Ten pounds?' he said, pulling the chain, 'You shall have it for five.'

Other people have stopped a train unwittingly. On more than one occasion, people unfamiliar with railway plumbing in the end compartment literally 'pulled the chain' to their later embarrassment. This happened to a visiting Russian dancer, the train shuddering to a standstill just outside of Gloucester.

In 1958 a girl aged seven made a serious mistake which caused 300 passengers on a London to Norwich express to be late.

'It was a matter of chains,' explained Guard Victor Bloom. 'Somebody pulled the communication cord, so I walked along the coach where the cord had been pulled. I found that it had been pulled inside a toilet. When I rapped on the door out darted a frightened little kiddie, almost in tears.'

'I pulled and pulled and pulled, and I can't make the lavatory go,' she gasped, as she ran past the guard. She was red in the face with her efforts and having to explain such a delicate situation.

In earlier days people mistook the chain as a control for other gadgets. One man pulled the cord on a London & North Western Railway express in mistake of a gas lamp chain, while another stopped a Great Northern express because he was cold and believed the chain controlled the heat. One lady even stopped a train because she had seen an attractive-looking house to let.

During the Second World War the Somerset & Dorset line was vital in carrying troops to the south coast ready for the D-Day landings. One troop train kept stopping because the soldiers failed to realise that hanging their kit bags on the chain made the train come to a halt.

Before the days of communication cords, the GWR broad gauge engines had iron shelters fixed to the rear of their tenders. These held a man facing rearwards who could see that nothing went amiss. The opponents of the broad gauge always referred to this watchman as 'the man in the iron coffin'.

One of the earliest communication systems was tested on the Bristol to Portishead branch in 1874. The mechanism, designed by Reuben Lyon of Bristol, was fixed to three coaches. It consisted of a bellows and a handle fixed to each compartment. By pulling down a handle, air was blown from a bellows through a pipe to the guard's van and also the engine where it blew whistles inserted into the ends of the pipe. In addition to this, the handle raised a signal arm, or a light at night, to indicate the compartment in which the apparatus had been used. The arm was so placed that it could not be lowered when the train was in motion. The pipe doubled as a speaking tube between the guards, or between a guard and a driver. The inventor tried it with 300 feet of tube, equivalent to ten or twelve coaches and the six whistles invariably worked.

A Wonderful Opportunity

Charles Richardson Wainwright, haberdasher of Euston Road, was sitting quietly in his compartment near the rear of the train as it drew out of Paddington.

Suddenly he saw an agitated man in uniform gesticulating wildly to him. It was the guard who was being left behind. The beautiful thought then dawned in Wainwright's mind that he was actually being implored to pull the emergency cord.

Curious Coincidence

In the nineteenth century Richard Pike travelled by the early morning mail train from the Midlands to the West of England. He recorded:

> At Taunton I perceived a crowd of persons gathered at the front of the train. I went forward and saw a corpse was being removed from the van to a hearse outside the station. On reading the inscription on the coffin plate, I was somewhat taken aback to find my own name. So Richard Pike living, and Richard Pike dead, had been travelling by the same train.

Curious Dimensions

The first GWR broad gauge horseboxes were very rough-riding – their width was shorter than their breadth!

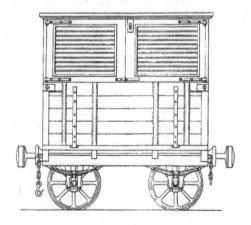

82. A short, broad gauge horsebox.

Travelling Post Offices

Travelling Post Offices (TPOs) were specially designed carriages fitted out as mobile sorting offices either attached to or forming trains. Sorting was carried out while the train was in motion.

The first such TPO was in January 1838 when the Post Office had a horsebox converted experimentally as a primitive sorting carriage and coupled to a train on the Grand Junction Railway between Birmingham and Warrington. Apparatus which enabled mail to be picked up and dropped while the trains were in motion also came into being that year. Early TPOs were austere – lit by oil lamps and without heating, or toilet facilities.

83. A mail train: the first coach carries a net to collect at speed, bags from a lineside post.

During both world wars TPOs did not run. After the Second World War, changes in the postal service ruled out the need for daytime TPOs. From 1968 when the two-tier letter post was introduced, TPOs only carried first class mail.

The principal Down night services working out of London were intended to provide a connection with the first delivery in England and Wales and wherever possible, next day delivery in Scotland for the main London evening postings. The equivalent Up services from the provinces were timed to connect with the first delivery in London districts and many other places. Cross-country and feeder TPOs were linked with the main routes to provide countrywide TPO coverage. By the time a train arrived at its destination, all the mail handled by the TPO was sorted into bundles for individual post offices and sometimes divided even further.

The Post Office paid BR to build and maintain its fleet of TPO vehicles and run them to schedules suitable for postal purposes.

In addition to the TPOs, the Post Office used Bag Tenders. These were Post Office vehicles but no sorting was carried out on board. Closed mail bags were only carried, accompanied by a small number of staff for loading and unloading.

During the Christmas period it was not practical to sort letters on board trains due to the vast amount of mail posted at this time. TPOs were suspended and most run as Bag Tenders.

The exchange of mail bags by line-side apparatus ceased in 1971.

It was possible to post first class letters on all TPOs – posting boxes being provided on the exterior of the coaches and at some principal stations, special late posting boxes were also situated on the platforms or nearby.

Scottish Special Trains

Harry Rosslyn, an English gambler, made a practice of hiring a special when he missed a scheduled train and when fishing in the Tay, he also hired a special from the North British Railway from Perth to Dysart where he lived, in order that his wife could enjoy his newly caught salmon that same evening.

Palnure on the Port Patrick & Wigtownshire Joint Railway served Cairnsmore on the Duke of Bedford's estate. The line, owned by the London & North Western Railway, Midland Railway, Caledonian Railway and Glasgow & South Western Railway, was unique for a Scottish railway in that it was partly under the ownership of an English railway.

An army of servants filled the house during the season and a daily special train travelled from London to Palnure carrying food for the duke's guests. His Grace, for some reason, did not care for the local water, so the train also conveyed drinking and washing water from south of the border.

Scooter Craze

In 1957 motor scooters were the latest craze. With over 150,000 motor scooters in Great Britain, the Western Region of BR believed there was a market to enable riders to enjoy twelve hours of travel in North Wales.

Departure from Paddington was at 12.30 a.m. on 1 September 1957 and the train arrived at Shrewsbury at 6.03 a.m. The return left Shrewsbury at 7.25 p.m. and arrived at Paddington at 11.15 p.m.

The specially-equipped vans held 100 scooters and the machines were allowed to have full tanks. There was also accommodation on the train for 200 passengers. The fare for rider and machine was £2, or for rider, machine and pillion passenger £3.

Commuters' Special

In 1935 Stuart Hibberd, the BBC's chief announcer, and five other passengers found after midnight that they had missed the last train from Charing Cross to Chislehurst as it had left without warning from a different platform. The marooned six went dismally to London Bridge station where Stuart Hibberd interviewed the station authorities and mentioned that he had just finished his duty for the day at Broadcasting House.

Presently a special train consisting of three coaches drew into the station and carried the six passengers to Chislehurst and for this working the whole line had to be kept electrified for an extra half an hour.

Trippers' Special

A cheap day trip was organised from Nailsworth, Gloucestershire, to Portsmouth. Four passengers from Nailsworth returned from the outing, but as the main line train was late, they arrived at Stonehouse after the last branch train had left for Nailsworth.

Asking the stationmaster what they should do, they received the reply 'Walk'. After observing that as they had purchased a return ticket, they considered it the railway's duty to return them to Nailsworth, the stationmaster rang Gloucester Control, omitting to inform them the number of passengers. Gloucester sent a train of three or four coaches to take just the four passengers to Nailsworth. The Stonehouse stationmaster had to ring his counterparts at all the branch stations to alert them to work the crossing gates and signals.

Camp Coaches

With the improvement of the standard of living, when more people were able to take a week or so off work to go on holiday, the railways introduced camping coaches. These were old passenger stock adapted for sleeping and living accommodation, the railway supplying bedding and crockery. Station toilets were used, holidaymakers being given a special key so that they did not have to pay a penny each time. Camp coaches were placed in attractive spots and were particularly handy if the campers took advantage of a weekly runabout ticket. A condition of using a camp coach was that it had to be reached by rail. The GWR introduced camping coaches at Easter 1934. Withdrawn during the Second World War, they were restored following the end of hostilities and by 1957 eight-berth coaches had a weekly rental varying from £7 in the low season to £11 10s in the high season.

Carriages on Inter-Company Workings

For the convenience of passengers, coaches worked over other companies' tracks. As far back as 1864, GWR carriages could be seen at Dover and South Eastern Railway carriages seen at Birkenhead when they formed a through train, each company supplying a set on alternate days. Since 1888 trains composed of GWR and LMS (or its predecessors) stock alternately ran between Penzance, Plymouth, Torquay, Swansea, Cardiff and Liverpool, Manchester, Carlisle and Glasgow.

In 1906 a train ran between Paddington and Brighton via Kensington. One particularly interesting 'foreign' working was in June 1866 when the morning broad gauge train from Windsor, before running over the broad gauge Metropolitan

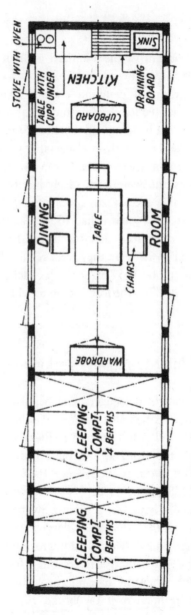

84. Plan of a 1930s GWR camp coach.

Railway rails to the City, slipped coaches at Paddington. The vehicles freewheeled into the GWR terminus where they were due three minutes after the main train had passed the through platforms at Bishop's Road, Paddington.

An Advertising Train

Manufacturers and traders always sought new ways of advertising and in 1933 the chocolate manufacturers J. S. Fry & Sons Ltd, with the cooperation of the GWR, used a travelling show train.

It was found that the most practical length was to use a train of three coaches; one for the exhibition, another for the salesmen's sleeping accommodation and the third containing an oil-driven generator to provide power for lighting and cooking.

The coaches to be used by Messrs Fry were stripped by the GWR of all internal fittings and handed over to Fry's, which arranged for them to be fitted and redecorated as desired, the firm opting to paint and letter the outside of the coaches and roof label boards. When the coaches were finished and fully stocked, the GWR required them to be insured by the promoter.

A tour of the principal towns was arranged and detailed timetables planned. The coaches usually moved during the night by express trains, thus maximising the daylight hours. On arrival at a town, the train was berthed in an easily accessible portion of the passenger, or goods station, and thrown open for inspection by customers who had received invitations. The main purpose of the show train was to draw customers' attention to ranges of goods which it would normally be difficult to bring to their notice, and additionally, to attract potential customers by inviting them to accept the firm's hospitality. Retail trading was not normally carried out from the train.

The charge for moving the train was based on the rate for conveying loaded vans, while reduced rates were charged for conveying Fry's staff.

Keep Out

A London banker whose frugality had something to do with the size of his fortune, always travelled third class, yet always managed to have a compartment for himself.

His method of keeping privacy had the simplicity of a genius. Whenever a train stopped at a platform he stood up, leaned out of the window, then, with a crooked finger and crafty smile, beckoned passengers into his compartment. Seeing his actions, even the bravest of travellers always hastened to find a seat elsewhere.

Why Whelks Are More Important than People

In the early 1960s, passengers on the 10.08 a.m. through train from Wells-on-Sea to King's Lynn sometimes had to change at Dereham when the train carried a large load of whelks needing to be delivered to Norwich. The reason that whelks were given more consideration than passengers was because it was easier to ask the passengers to change trains, rather than shift the whelks, so the shellfish had the benefit of a through journey.

Passengers' Luggage

In 1959 Geoffrey Moss, of Eye, Suffolk, was stopped as he stepped off his train at Norwich. As usual he had been holding a guitar between his knees in the compartment. An inspector informed him: 'A guitar is not personal hand-luggage on an outward journey by cheap-day ticket – although it may be on the return journey.'

The guitar was found to weigh 12 lbs and Geoffrey ordered to pay an excess luggage charge of 2*s* 7*d*. A railway official said: 'We were within the regulations, but will turn a blind eye to the guitar in future. A day-return passenger may take only personal hand-luggage on the outward journey. On the return, a passenger may carry more baggage – up to 60 lb in weight – to cover possible purchases.'

A Conversation at Paddington

A scene one day at Paddington –
Ticket collector: That your sewing machine, Ma'am?
Passenger: Yes.
Ticket collector: Then you left a pie on it.
Passenger: I left a pie on it?
Ticket collector: Yes, you left a pie on it.
Passenger: But I didn't. It wasn't my pie … Oh! You mean I'll have to pay?
Ticket collector: Yes, you left a pie.

Claim Against the North British Railway

At Falkirk sheriff court on 15 February 1914, Sheriff-Substitute Moffatt gave judgment in a claim against the North British Railway for £10 worth of damages.

A female passenger had placed luggage on the rack, was standing at the door of her compartment facing the platform and about to reach for an umbrella and waterproof which her mother was holding out for her, when a porter, without warning,

85. Platform 1, Paddington.

came quickly forward and slammed the carriage door, severely crushing her right thumb.

The North British Railway denied fault and pleaded contributory negligence on the part of the pursuer. The Sheriff found that fault on the North British Railway was not established. 'It could not be said to be the duty of porters in shutting carriage doors to make a careful examination of the inside of the carriages to see if any part of any passenger's person was in danger of injury from the action of the door.'

Drama on a Special Train

On 5 December 1872 a case, Glenie versus the GWR, was heard in the Court of Common Pleas. It was an action to recover damages from an injury received on 3 January 1872.

Mr Glenie was travelling in a special train from Reading to Paddington, put on for those who had attended the Reading Steeplechase meeting. About twenty minutes after the train had left Reading, a loud report was heard, followed by a violent oscillation of the coach caused by a snapping leaf spring.

Glenie and others pulled the communication cord, but the string came into the compartment loose. Using their wits, they cogitated and thought of the idea of lighting newspapers and throwing them out. This failed to attract the attention of the driver, but the guard saw the flaming journals and pulled the cord to sound the driver's gong. The train stopped near West Drayton and the defective coach was shunted into a siding.

Mr Glenie was manager and publisher of the *Stage* magazine, but in consequence of the shock to his system caused by the breaking of the spring, he suffered from sickness, pain in the head, dizziness, loss of memory and unfitness for work, the journal having to fold after only four issues.

The GWR said that the coaches had been properly examined before starting and that the leaf broke from some 'latent undiscoverable defect' for which the company could not be answerable. It said that the communication cord was in perfect order on the off side of the train in accordance with regulations, (the alarm gong was fitted on the off side), but the other side was only in use when going the other way. (Seemingly Glenie and the other passengers had pulled the nearside cord.)

The question was put to Glenie that the injury caused by the accident was not as serious as he claimed, but had been caused by a previous injury.

The jury considered for almost four hours and then came up with a verdict in the GWR's favour.

Scotland Yard

During the First World War, Sir Edward Henry, Commissioner of Police at Scotland Yard, ceased to ride on horseback to his office and used the underground railway, often taking his dog with him.

On one occasion, an inspector stopped him and asked for his ticket for the dog. Sir Edward said that he did not think that the dog needed a ticket; in fact, he did not know that the dog was there and it must have followed him from his home. The inspector gave him a warning and noted his name and address.

Two days later Sir Edward received a complimentary 'life' season ticket made out to 'Sir Edward Henry's dog' from the underground head office.

Escalator Trouble

In the 1930s when escalators were new, it seemed that all eyes on a crowded escalator were turned to a delightful-looking old couple: he with a snow-white beard and looking very spick and span, and she very demure in black.

They were just standing side by side and someone was heard to remark: 'What a dear old Darby and Joan'. Someone else, standing closer, thought so too until she reached the top and waiting for them to move off the escalator heard the old lady say: 'You got me on the bloody thing; now you can get me orf!'

You Must Obey the Sign

The brevity of London Passenger Transport Board's warning notice at escalators, 'Dogs must be carried', must have seriously confused passengers – where were they going to find one? A later version of the sign exhorted a passenger to carry both dog *and* a pushchair!

The Sick Thief

Asked why he had robbed the same building no less than five times, the captured thief explained: 'I've got a heart condition and can't run far. This office is near the underground station.'

Making Use of the Facilities

When the Inner Circle line was steam worked, the side tanks of Metropolitan & District engines became so hot as a result of condensing the exhaust steam that the water tanks had to be emptied and refilled.

Engine crews discovered a use for their hot water. To boil a fish they twisted a wire round its tail and hooked it over the neck of the filling orifice. The train guard was granted use of this cooking facility, but if he had upset the locomotive crew it was deliberately left in too long so that when he came to collect it, it was just a skeleton on wire.

Underground men also adopted the common practice of frying eggs and bacon on a shovel, but the use of the blower to create a draught had to be deferred, or the meal was dragged off the shovel and went up the chimney in smoke.

A Little Knowledge Is a Dangerous Thing

The fine bronze memorial on the Embankment depicting Samuel Plimsoll meant nothing to two girls. Suddenly light dawned when one noticed the embossed Plimsoll mark above the great man's name. Pointing triumphantly to the familiar bisected circle she proudly exclaimed: 'Of course, it's the man who started London Transport!'

Suicide Preventer

By 1926 it was recognized that tube stations formed favourite sites for suicides – in fact so many occurred that the underground railway companies tried to prevent, or at least, reduce them.

On the Morden line, opened in 1926, a pit, 1 foot 4 inches in depth was provided between the running rails throughout the length of each station, while on extensions to the Piccadilly line, a 2-foot-deep pit was constructed and the platforms carried on arches to permit staff to get underneath a train.

The comparative absence of suicides on those sections showed the value of the arrangement and in 1935 all London underground stations were provided with 2-foot-deep pits. Suicides became fewer and the delays occasioned by them were greatly reduced.

Can Railways Affect Climate?

Railways can be affected by climate, but can climate be affected by railways? It is believed on good authority that the Metropolitan Railway did when it ran into the foothills of the Chilterns and crossed on a fairly high embankment, pierced by a low and narrow outlet, a somewhat deep and narrow valley running north and then west.

When the line was first constructed, the whole of the area was open country, but then E. L. Hawke, secretary of the Royal Meteorological Society, came to live there and started taking readings. It soon appeared that the climatic conditions, as to temperature, were peculiar and almost unique. The place showed all the characteristics of a 'valley climate' in an extreme form. Frosts were very frequent and on cold nights the temperature fell faster and lower than anywhere in the district or county. On clear, calm nights, the cold air flowed down the sides of the valley and became coldest at the bottom, dispersing where the lowest level opened out. Here the Metropolitan Railway came in and prevented such dispersal, the embankment acting like a dam to a reservoir and impounded the cold air like water in a pond. Had the gap been bridged, instead of being crossed by a solid embankment, much of the cold air would have escaped and the record low temperatures at night and the increased temperature on a warm day due to the enclosed position would not have been achieved.

86. A 1922 Metropolitan Railway advertisement.

In 1935, Rothamsted had a maximum temperature of 84 degrees Fahrenheit and a minimum of 13 degrees, whereas corresponding figures at Rickmansworth were 89 degrees and 7 degrees.

The mean daily range of temperature at Rickmansworth, which exceeded 21 degrees over the year, was probably greater than at any other location in England, and for this condition there could be little doubt that the railway embankment was responsible.

Underground Shelters Don't Protect You from Everything

During the bombing raids on London of the Second World War, people used tube shelters at night as air-raid shelters. They found, rather surprisingly, that they were bitten by mosquitoes.

87. A London tube train.

These insects were first discovered there in 1936, having bred in stagnant water in the tunnels. It was thought to be a simple matter to exterminate larvae by oiling the pools, so the London Passenger Transport Board set to work, but the mosquitoes flourished and spread.

With or Without an Apostrophe?

In 1956 the *Manchester Guardian* wrote:

> Almost unnoticed by the public, a number of London underground stations have for some time been living in a state of double identity. King's Cross, Earl's Court, St Paul's, and Regent's Park, for instance, take an apostrophe before their final "s" in all maps and other printed publicity, but no apostrophe on metal name-plates and indicator boards.
>
> The explanation is that when the old London Passenger Transport Board worked out modern designs for its publicity, it dropped the apostrophe for the sake of simplicity and clarity; but since the early 1950s it has been gradually slipping the apostrophe back into names that suggest possession.

88. Earls Court and Kings Cross tickets without an apostrophe.

London Transport is also taking the occasion to do away with inconsistencies. One station which used to appear as 'St. James Park' on maps and 'St James' Park' on the station nameplate, will eventually appear everywhere as 'St James's Park'.

The new system makes for some nice distinctions. Where Earl has possession his court – and therefore an apostrophe – Barons Court has neither. Parsons (of the Green), and Rayners (of the Lane), also remain without apostrophes. Perhaps it all has to do with the retreat from the extreme kind of functionalism, though no one has gone so far as Bernard Shaw, he spelled it 'Earlscourt'.

Carriage Heating

Until the end of the nineteenth century, passengers had to rely on foot-warmers – metal tins filled with hot water and supplied at a charge. In the 1880s F. W. Webb of the London & North Western Railway patented foot-warmers containing a solution of soda acetate. These were heated at the stations and as the solution re-crystallised, it gave off heat. This was modified by having soda acetate-filled radiators in carriages being supplied with steam periodically. Other systems were either hot water or steam from the engine being circulated through the coaches. The low pressure steam system was the one generally adopted. This meant that the early diesel locomotives were required to have steam-heating boilers and it looked odd to see steam emanating from a diesel engine. From 1964 all new coaches were electrically heated.

Two into One Will Go

During the heavy air raids on London in the autumn of 1940, a District trailer car was hit and badly damaged, three-quarters of its length being almost destroyed, but one part of the coach remained almost untouched.

As it stood, the car was hardly worth repairing, but a week or so later, by a strange coincidence another car of similar type, a Metropolitan motor car was also hit. This time only one end was wrecked.

As cars were impossible to replace in wartime, it was suggested that it might be worth the attempt to make one good car from the two wrecked vehicles. Glass for the windows was the largest single item needing replacement.

Carriage Lighting

Coach lighting in the early days of railways was simply to make darkness visible. In third class one light often had to serve the whole coach. Even in a first class carriage the oil lamp in the roof was not of sufficient power to enable one to read. To do this passengers carried a candle on a spiked holder and stuck this into the upholstery, running the risk of greasing both their clothes and the fabric.

In the late 1850s railways began to adopt gas lighting, some using coal gas, but most preferring oil gas obtained from shale oil. Oil was fed by gravitation to a red-hot retort where it was vaporised, condensed to a gas holder and piped to carriage sidings. Coaches had a cylinder of rubber and canvas on the underframe for storage. Each reservoir could store sufficient gas for twenty lights burning from twenty to twenty-four hours. The danger with gas lighting was that in the event of a serious derailment, the gas, combined with rolling stock mainly built of timber, gave rise to an even worse disaster as happened at Quintinshill on 22 May 1915 when at least 227 were killed and 246 injured in Britain's worst railway accident.

Train Cruises

One innovation in 1933 was the Northern Belle train cruise. This far-sighted move drew public attention to the scenic possibilities of the railways in addition to being a commercial venture.

The purely financial results of the enterprise vindicated the confidence which had inspired it and quite a few of the passengers who patronised the train in 1934 were those who had done so the previous year.

The fifteen-coach train provided accommodation for sixty passengers and a staff of twenty-seven. Where convenient, the night portion of the train, including six first class sleeping cars, was detached and worked separately. The day coaches provided quarters for the staff, a kitchen car, two restaurant cars, a hairdressing saloon, ladies retiring room, buffet and office, and writing and smoking rooms.

In 1934 the Northern Belle left King's Cross at 9.00 p.m. on Friday 1 June and travelled to Barnard Castle. On Sunday it reached Penrith from where a motor coach tour took passengers to the Lake District. Monday was devoted to excursions in the Edinburgh area. On Tuesday Royal Deeside and Braemar were visited by motor coach from Aberdeen and at 11.00 p.m. the train left for Balloch Pier. The journey up Loch Lomond was made by steamer on Wednesday morning and passengers rejoined the day coaches of the train at Ardlui, before travelling to Fort William where the night portion had been sent ahead from Balloch Pier and was awaiting them.

On Wednesday afternoon the day coaches travelled to Mallaig and back over the West Highland line. As this journey included some of the finest railway scenery in the British Isles, and the Northern Belle stopped on Glenfinnan Viaduct to allow passengers to enjoy the view up the glen and down Loch Shiel, it may have explained why the majority of the passengers preferred

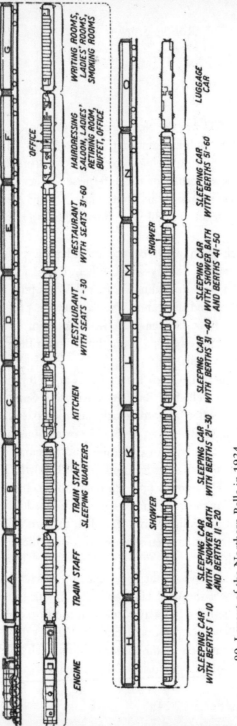

ENGINE

TRAIN STAFF

TRAIN STAFF
SLEEPING QUARTERS

KITCHEN

RESTAURANT
WITH SEATS 1 - 30

RESTAURANT
WITH SEATS 31-60

HAIRDRESSING
SALOON, LADIES'
RETIRING ROOM,
BUFFET, OFFICE

WRITING ROOMS,
LADIES' ROOMS,
SMOKING ROOMS

OFFICE

SLEEPING CAR
WITH BERTHS 1 - 10

SLEEPING CAR
WITH SHOWER BATH
AND BERTHS 11 - 20

SHOWER

SLEEPING CAR
WITH BERTHS 21 - 30

SLEEPING CAR
WITH BERTHS 31 - 40

SLEEPING CAR
WITH SHOWER BATH
AND BERTHS 41 - 50

SHOWER

SLEEPING CAR
WITH BERTHS 51 - 60

LUGGAGE
CAR

89. Layout of the Northern Belle in 1934.

to take that option rather than the alternative motor coach tour to Fort Augustus, with the problematical, and incidentally unfulfilled, view of the Loch Ness monster.

On Thursday morning the day portion proceeded to Craigendoran where passengers embarked on the SS *Waverley* for a sail down the Firth of Clyde and round the Kyles of Bute. After returning to Craigendoran, passengers were taken to Edinburgh, leaving at 12.05 a.m. on Friday and arriving back at King's Cross at 10.45 a.m.

As a variant to meals on the train, dinner was served at LNER hotels during the visits to Edinburgh and Aberdeen. On three nights out of the seven the train was stationary and on the other four it was at rest for part of the time. The Northern Belle made four cruises in the June 1934 season and its accommodation at £20 a head was fully booked for all of them. Only the exigencies of summer traffic working prevented its extension through the later holiday months.

The LNER Takes You Up in the World

In 1934 some of the latest rolling stock exhibitions of the LNER in aid of hospitals and other charities, in addition to advertising the railway itself, included some diverting sideshows, one being an open goods wagon demounted from its wheels. Visitors were then invited to enter the wagon which was seized by a breakdown crane in steam, then lifted, swung gently round through a complete circle and deposited on the ground again.

At the modest price of 2*d* a head for adults and 1*d* for children the 'Ascent to the Stratosphere' as it was called, was continuously in demand. The maximum number of passengers on one lift was seventy-three, thus handsomely beating the 'Chevaux 8 Hommes 40' of the French First World War box wagons.

The Origin of the GWR Colours of Chocolate and Cream

GWR carriages were painted brown all over until October 1864 when the directors decided that the upper parts of the carriages of all classes should be painted white. When varnished this produced a cream tint. Cream and brown remained the livery until 1909, when it was decided to revert to brown all over. One train had been painted dark lake experimentally in 1903 and in 1912 the brown livery changed to crimson lake which lasted for ten years until the chocolate and cream were made once more the standard colours.

Upholstery

In the early days of railways, first class carriages were generally upholstered, but the second class had to be content with bare wooden seats until about 1860. About ten years later the bare wooden seats and backs of the third class were gradually covered with upholstery and before the end of the nineteenth century the only difference between the second and third class accommodation was the provision of a strip of carpet in the former.

The abolition of second class by the Midland Railway in 1875 meant that ex-second class compartments became third and so third class passengers could enjoy upholstered seating.

New Is Not Always Best

The following critical letter appeared in the December 1959 issue of *Trains Illustrated*:

Sir, – I should like to enquire what steps are taken by the Ministry of Transport to ensure that passenger vehicles maintain a certain standard of comfort. I may be unlucky in my choice of trains, but the new 12-car long-distance Kent Coast electrics on which I have travelled have had riding characteristics so incredibly bad that I wonder if something should not be done to have a question asked in the new Parliament. Although I have served in destroyers and small ships I have never until now experienced a form of travel sickness which leaves a 24-hour "hangover". By the time the train reached Ramsgate from London I thought I had got used to the vicious rock, roll, pitch and uninhibited gyration of the coach; but on alighting I could hardly walk straight and failed to do justice to my supper. As this was my third journey on these boneshakers I am beginning to think there must be some very serious fault in their design. It is not true to say that all multiple-unit stock suffers from these troubles.

Multiple-unit diesels, underground trains – even the Portuguese light railway electric trains – are far smoother running. And it is not just my reactions either. Kent Coast residents complain bitterly of the impossibility of using the buffet cars once the train is in motion; and I find the steam trains which go to Ramsgate via Dover and Deal delightfully comfortable by comparison. Of course they take longer; but who wants to spend their first day at the seaside recovering from train-sickness? Finally, if you were a foreign visitor arriving at Dover after a rough channel crossing and you then found the train to London was, if anything, worse than the boat in a heavy swell, how long would it be before you changed to air travel?

However, I recently travelled from Victoria to Ramsgate in a train composed of four-car sets, and to my pleasant surprise the coaches behaved very well indeed. It was possible to read a newspaper and even to doze off to sleep. Apparently it is only the six-car sets which ride like bucking broncos.

W. A. Corkill

Ambulance Trains

During both world wars the principal railway companies produced ambulance trains. One of those created by the GWR was exhibited at Paddington in August 1915, a relatively high charge of a shilling being made and the money collected, including that from the sale of packets of postcards illustrating the train and some of its vehicles, being given for the benefit of the wounded and for railwaymen serving in the forces.

In the First World War the Midland & South Western Junction Railway carried endless streams of hospital trains from Southampton to the north and in the 1960s old people were still saying: 'Them trains never stopped.' Regular runs were made with wounded from Dieppe and Cherbourg, some men still plastered with Flanders mud. Drivers were so busy working the ambulance trains that they did not see their families for a fortnight at a time, occasionally even working twenty-four hours without a rest.

The first MSWJR ambulance trains were allotted only one engine and sometimes stalled on a gradient. On one occasion a doctor told the guard that the efforts of the driver to get the engine up the slope had thrown seven men off their stretchers. Later, two engines were used, the London & South Western engine, usually a 4-4-0, and a Midland & South Western engine placed in front as pilot.

During the Second World War ambulance trains were generally hauled by LNER 4-6-0 B12/3 class engines which had wide route availability and could pass over most of the lines in the country.

Slip Coaches

Slip coaches were an invention which enabled a coach to be detached from a train without the need for it to be stopped, thus speeding working.

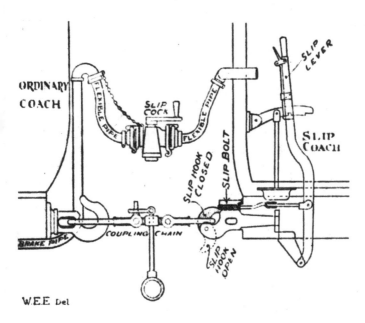

90. Details of a slip coach apparatus.

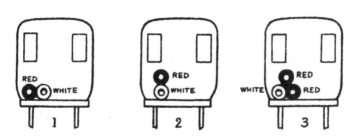

FIG. 18.—Slip Coach Tail Lamps.

1.—One " Slip " only.　　2.—Rearmost of two Slip portions.
3.—Rearmost of three Slip portions.

91. Slip coach tail lamps.

92. Slipping coaches: the main train is on the left, while the two coaches on the left have been slipped.

Approaching the station where his coach was to be slipped, the slip guard would lean out of the his front window and unfasten the brake and heating pipes, then pull a lever which caused the coupling hook to drop, thus detaching his carriage from the main train. He was able to control the brakes and bring it to a halt in the platform.

Sometimes the inevitable happened, he braked too soon and the coach stopped short of the platform. In this case a shunting horse, or an engine if available, would be sent to collect it.

10

Miscellany

Road Services

The GWR was the pioneer of railway-operated passenger road services in Britain. As early as 1903 it introduced a bus service between Helston and the Lizard, while another service was started shortly afterwards between Penzance and Marazion. These and other services were introduced as feeders to the railway.

In 1928 the Big Four obtained parliamentary powers to own and operate road services for both passengers and goods, but it was decided to follow a policy of cooperation rather than competition with existing bus undertakings. Within approximately two years of the passing of the Act, the railway companies transferred all their passenger road fleet to the principal bus companies operating in their territory and had acquired a financial interest not exceeding 50 per cent in the undertakings.

Another important outcome of the 1928 powers was the acquisition in 1930, jointly with the other main line companies, of Carter Paterson & Co and Hays Wharf Cartage Co. which embraced Messrs Pickfords.

93. A London & North Western
Railway road motor car ticket.

94. A GWR road motor car ticket.

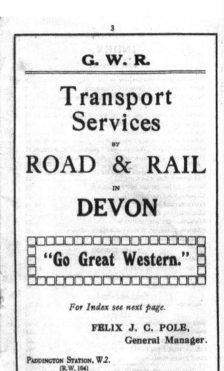

G.W.R. ROAD MOTOR CAR SERVICES.

GENERAL NOTICES AND REGULATIONS.

TABLES.—The Company gives notice that the Road Motor vices are run subject to the conditions of roads and circumstances ing, and that the times are approximate and liable to alteration. mpany does not undertake that the cars shall either start or at the time specified in the Time Tables, or that there shall cient room in the cars to accommodate intending passengers r luggage ; and the Company will not be accountable for any convenience, or injury, which may arise from delay or detention ny cause whatsoever.

occasions when snow or fog prevails, or the state of the roads is lly difficult, it may be necessary to vary the times of the Road Cars, or to suspend the running of certain services without notice.

ENGERS.—Train passengers and passengers for the more distant on the car route will, so far as is REASONABLY PRACTICABLE, be reference over persons desiring to travel short distances only. cars will call to pick up or set down passengers at the fare stages in the Time Tables. Passengers may also join the cars at other en route on payment of the fare from the previous stage. Intend- ssengers are requested to give a clear and distinct signal to the of their desire for the car to stop.

ENGERS' TICKETS. Passengers, **on entering the Company's** otors are requested to obtain tickets (punched in their presence) ange for fares paid ; also to see that they are given a ticket to uggage charges, etc. Conductors will punch tickets in the stage r to which the passenger is entitled to travel. Passengers are to verify the stage number so indicated by means of the Fare xhibited in all Cars. Tickets must be retained until completion journey and produced for inspection on the request of an official Company. Tickets are not transferable.

URN TICKETS are issued between many of the principal places road routes at reduced rates. Return Tickets are available for journey for an indefinite period. These tickets must be retained ir entirety by the passenger and surrendered to the Conductor on turn journey, when an Exchange Ticket will be issued in exchange. cases where Return Tickets are not operative, **BOOKS OF 12 E JOURNEY TICKETS** (transferable and available on any G.W. Motor Car Service) can be obtained at Stations from which Road Car Services operate, at the following reduced rates :—1d. tickets, 2d. tickets, 1/9 ; 3d. tickets, 2/7½ ; 4d. tickets, 3/6 ; 5d. tickets, 6d. tickets, 5/3 ; and at proportionate rates for tickets over value

OKS OF 12 SCHOLARS' AND APPRENTICES' (SINGLE NEY TICKETS) available for properly accredited scholars and ntices up to 18 years of age, are issued at half rates. viz., when the ary single adult fare is 2d., 1/- ; 3d., 1/6 ; 4d., 2/- ; 5d., 2/6 ; - ; and at proportionate rates for tickets over 6d. in value.

ASON TICKETS at reduced rates are issued to Adult Scholars and entices on certain routes. Application should be made to the Stationmaster.

ILDREN.—Children over 3 years of age and under 12 years are d at approximately half single fares. Children under 3 years of re carried free of charge.

Company desires to run the car services as efficiently and punctually sible. Passengers can materially assist by entering and leaving the quickly. Passengers are warned not to enter or leave cars in motion. gestions from the public for the improvement or extension of ar Services will be welcomed and carefully considered.

95. GWR Road Motor Services booklet for 9 July 1928.

Railway Air Services

In 1929 the Big Four obtained parliamentary powers enabling them to operate air services. In Europe they were only able to operate as far as longitude twenty degrees east of Greenwich; this enabled the potential of railway air services to Iceland, Ireland and Portugal, but cut it off from serving Sweden and Norway north of the Gulf of Bothnia, while a good deal of Poland, Hungary and the Balkans was also excluded from the operating area.

The GWR was the first company to take the initiative and on 12 April 1933 inaugurated a service between Cardiff, Haldon (sited just inland from Dawlish and thus serving Teignmouth and Torquay) and Plymouth. The plane, a three-engined, six-seater Westland Wessex, built appropriately in GWR territory at Yeovil, was painted in chocolate and cream livery.

Imperial Airways supplied the plane, pilot and ground staff for the twice daily flights. It took about fifty minutes to cover the 80 miles, compared with almost four hours and 140 miles by rail. The GWR provided buses to connect with Cardiff General, Torquay and Plymouth North Road stations and the enquiry bureau at Teignmouth Town Hall. On 22 May 1933 the service was extended to Birmingham. Despite a substantial traffic response and the sale of railway air mail stamps, the service lost £6,526 in its first season.

In 1934 the four main line railway companies, in association with Imperial Airways, formed the Railway Air Services Limited. The SR sponsored a service between Croydon and the Isle of Wight, followed by the GWR introducing a Liverpool to Plymouth service. The LMS flew services between London, Birmingham, Manchester, Belfast and Glasgow. The LNER failed to sponsor any services as it was concentrating on 70 mph plus railway services.

In 1938 the Great Western Air Service and the Southern Air Service united to form the Great Western & Southern Air Service and thus eliminated competition on the Channel Island routes.

In 1944 the Big Four published a plan for the development of air transport to Europe. However the change to a Labour government in 1945 altered the ownership plan and brought an end to railway development in air transport. British European Airways took over the railway airlines on 1 April 1947 and the Railways Act of 1993 extinguished the 1929 air powers which BR had inherited in 1948.

Flying Boats

In July 1937 Imperial Airways developed a flying boat base at Southampton. Railway connections were provided from Waterloo when at least twice a week the 8.30 a.m. left Waterloo with one or two Pullman cars and a brake attached. This special brake bore roof boards: 'Imperial Airways Empire Service' and was detached at Southampton Central and worked to No. 50 berth where passengers and luggage were transferred to motor launches to be taken to the flying boat moorings in Southampton Water.

The flight clerk travelled in the van and was provided with a desk and weighing machine so that en route he could compute the load sheet for that particular flight. For the inbound services, the special portion was attached to any convenient train. By 1939 traffic had grown to such an extent that it was sufficient to run an independent train to and from Southampton.

Post Office Mails by Rail

The Post Office sent the bulk of its mail by road, until 4 February 1840 when a night mail train between Paddington and Twyford was established, also carrying passengers. The first sorting office carriages, four in number, were ordered by the postmaster general in July 1841 and four second class coaches were adapted to carry the day mail bags, as their guard sheltered from the weather.

On 1 February 1855 the first solely postal train in the world was introduced on the GWR between Paddington and Bristol. The Down train left Paddington at 8.46 p.m. and reached Bath 106¾ miles distant at 12.30 a.m., after seven intermediate stops. In the reverse direction the train left Bristol at 12.35 a.m. and reached Paddington at 4.10 a.m. The train was very light, generally consisting of two sorting carriages and a van. Officially known as the 'Special Mail', the staff referred to it as the 'Little Mail'.

The GWR Pioneers the Electric Telegraph

Among the many pioneering exploits of the GWR was the introduction of the electric telegraph, which could be claimed to be the grandfather of the many electrical communication devices in use today.

The system was certainly in operation by 6 April 1839. It reached Slough in 1843 and was made famous by its speedy announcement to London of the birth of Queen Victoria's second son on 6 August 1844.

The receiving apparatus consisted of a dial with five vertical magnetic needles. On the dial twenty letters were marked, the various letters being indicated by the convergence of two

100 YEARS OF PUBLIC SERVICE

GREAT WESTERN RAILWAY "**FIRSTS**"—

FIRST ROYAL TRAIN JOURNEY.
FIRST POSTAL TRAIN.
FIRST 'NON-STOP' EXPRESS Over 100 Miles.
FIRST LOCOMOTIVE TO EXCEED 100 m.p.h.
FIRST PASSENGER MOTOR OMNIBUS Service.
FIRST RAILWAY OPERATED AIR SERVICE.

Pioneers of Railway Electric Telegraph, Train Lighting by Electricity, Slip-Coach Working, Audible Cab Signalling for Automatic Train Control, Streamlined Locomotives, etc., . . .

AND STILL FOREMOST
WITH INNOVATIONS FOR INCREASING
SPEED — COMFORT — SAFETY.

96. In its centenary poster the GWR celebrates that it ran the first postal train.

needles. The communicator consisted of five longitudinal bars, each connected with a separate length of wire, and two transverse metal bars fixed on a wooden frame, the latter bars being connected with the poles of a battery. Two parallel rows of stops were fixed to the longitudinal bars, the depression of any two of which, situated in the opposite rows, formed metallic connection with the transverse bars below and caused a current to flow through the appropriate wires connected with the longitudinal bars. An alarm was provided to call the operator's attention when a message was to be sent.

In 1843 an improved system consisting of double-needle instruments and requiring only two wires was introduced between Paddington and Slough.

The first use of the telegraph for police purposes happened in 1844 on the Eton Montem Day, an occasion which had a special attraction for the light-fingered gentry.

In the telegraph book then kept at Paddington, passages were entered recording various messages forwarded from the terminus indicating the presence of known thieves on certain trains. Police

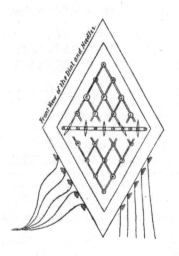

97. The dial of the electric magnetic telegraph which was installed on the GWR between Paddington and West Drayton in 1839.

Under the Special Patronage of Her Majesty

And H. R. H. **Prince Albert**

GALVANIC AND MAGNETO

ELECTRIC TELEGRAPH,

GT. WESTERN RAILWAY.

The Public are respectfully informed that this interesting & most extraordinary Apparatus, by which upwards of 50 SIGNALS can be transmitted to a Distance of 280,000 MILES in ONE MINUTE,

May be seen in operation, daily, (Sundays excepted,) from 9 till 8, at the

Telegraph Office, Paddington,

AND TELEGRAPH COTTAGE, SLOUGH.

ADMISSION 1s.

" *This Exhibition is well worthy a visit from all who love to see the wonders of science.*"—Morning Post.

Despatches instantaneously sent to and fro with the most confiding secrecy. Post Horses and Conveyances of every description may be ordered by the Electric Telegraph, to be in readiness on the arrival of a Train, at either Paddington or Slough Station.

The Terms for sending a Despatch, ordering Post Horses, &c., only One Shilling.

N.B. Messengers in constant attendance, so that communications received by Telegraph, would be forwarded, if required, to any part of London, Windsor, Eton, &c.

THOMAS HOME, *Licensee.*

G. NURTON, Printer, 48, Church Street, Portman Market.

98. Poster advertising the GWR's electric telegraph.

99. The telegraph cottage at Slough in 1844.

officials at Slough warned the suspects and made two arrests.
A message transmitted from Slough read:

> Slough, 11.51 am. Several of the suspected persons who came by
> the various Down trains are lurking about Slough, uttering bitter
> invectives against the telegraph. Not one of those cautioned has
> ventured to proceed to the Montem.

One female passenger lost her bag containing two sovereigns and
one of these was found in the watch fob of one of the thieves.

The Great Southern & Western Railway?

Following the railway construction mania of 1845–46, a deep
depression in trade occurred and had serious effects on the
financial position of the Great Western, London & North
Western and London & South Western companies.

The boards of these companies met in September 1848 for the
purpose of adopting some immediate measures for counteracting
the prejudicial effects on the railways, which had been occasioned
by the great demands for additional capital for many new lines.
They finally resolved on 1 November 1848 that the most effectual
plan would be an absolute and permanent amalgamation of the
three companies under an Act of Parliament, even settling the
preliminary arrangements. These conclusions were announced
to the shareholders, but ten days before the meetings which
had been called to ratify the resolutions, difficulties arose
about the terms, so this scheme, which would have so vitally
affected the future railway development of the country, was
dropped.

Escaped German Prisoners of War Captured at Newport

Smart work carried out by A. Johnson, a berthing man employed by the GWR at Newport Docks, led to the capture of two escaped German prisoners of war at Alexandra Docks, Newport in 1945.

Noticing two men loitering near No. 18 coal hoist at the South Dock, Mr Johnson became suspicious and telephoned the docks police who promptly sent officers to investigate. The men, who had taken refuge in an empty hut, were questioned and it was quickly established that they were escaped German prisoners. They were unarmed, but had in their possession emergency rations and cigarettes sufficient to last them some days, as well as a road map of England and Wales.

It was ascertained that one of the men had been a member of the German merchant navy service before the war. With his companion he had intended making for Cardiff Docks of which he had some knowledge and there boarding a vessel which would have enabled them to return to Germany. One of the fugitives was wearing an old GWR fawn mackintosh he had acquired.

GWR Radio Stations

One Second World War secret was the provision of radio communication introduced to ensure the continuance of telecommunications in the event of a breakdown of landlines due to enemy action. A network of radio stations was set up covering the whole of the GWR system with intercommunication facilities with similar networks of the other railway companies.

In 1940 experimental licences were issued by the postmaster general which enabled radio tests to be carried out between Paddington and Reading. On the successful completion of these tests, full transmitting and receiving licences were issued by the postmaster general. A complete network consisting of four fixed stations, nine rail mobile units and three road mobile units was planned.

The fixed stations were installed in specially-built brick and concrete buildings at Castle Bar, Radyr, Swindon and Aldermaston. The mobile units were situated at Severn Beach, Llantarnam, Skewen, Earlswood Lakes, Shrewsbury, Charlton Kings, Stoke Canon, Brent and Liskeard. Two road units were at Paddington and one at Gloucester.

Railway and Post Office telephone communication was provided in the fixed stations and rail mobile units and in the event of communication being completely broken, arrangements were made for a despatch rider service to be brought into operation for the conveyance of messages between divisional headquarters and the radio station.

All messages were to be signalled in morse and to ensure secrecy place names, phrases of a military character and information likely to be useful to the enemy had to be coded by means of a special cipher supplied by the security authorities.

The transmitting power of 20–25 watts gave a normal radiation of 40–50 miles. Sets in the fixed stations and mobile units were operated either by mains or battery, those in the road mobile units by battery only.

The rail mobile units were specially converted four-wheel passenger coaches. Each was fitted with a sleeping compartment for four persons. Heating and cooking facilities were provided by a coal stove and an electric heater/cooker. A supply of emergency rations was kept on hand for use in case of complete isolation of the unit. Washing facilities were available, water being carried in a tank in the roof.

King Coal

Coal-class traffic, which also included coke, patent fuel, for the whole of BR in 1957 was 166,153,300 tons, that is about half a million tons per day and approximately 60 per cent of the total freight traffic. Of these 166,153,300 tons, 43,546,800 tons originated in the North Eastern Region – the birthplace of English railways. As early as 1903 the North Eastern Railway adopted 20-ton wagons as standard, when elsewhere in the country most mine owners were using wagons carrying half, or even less, this weight. A train of 20-ton wagons held one third more coal than a train of the same weight consisting of 10½-ton wagons and only occupied four fifths of the space.

Wagon discharge was more efficient in the north east. Bottom door, or hopper discharge, had been a feature long before the adoption of the standard hopper wagon of 1903. It offered rapid wagon turnaround with quick discharge with the minimum amount of manual assistance. This was a contrast to South

100. Elevators in South Wales for raising coal wagons and tipping the contents into ships' holds.

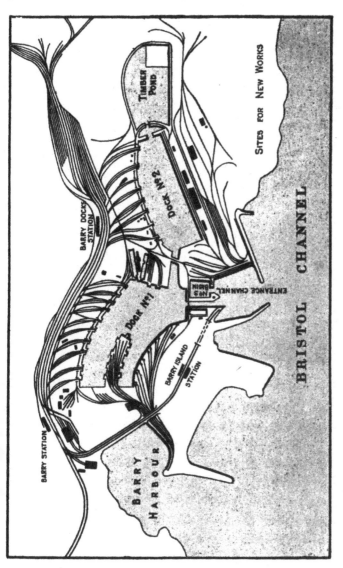

101. Nests of sidings at Barry Dock for the export of coal.

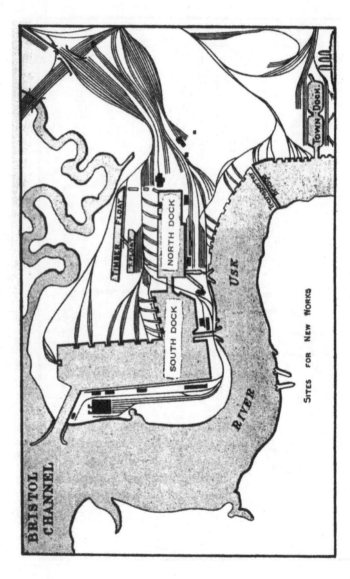

102. Nests of sidings at Newport for the export of coal.

Wales, where wagons were physically tipped; this process made them far more prone to damage and wagon examiners were required to keep a close watch in order to check that the brake gear, couplings and buffers, woodwork and strapping were in good order.

The coal cells at North Eastern stations were more efficient than the manual method used further south. Instantaneous discharge of coal from a hopper wagon into a cell not only dispensed with the manual unloading and stacking of coal, but also speeded up wagon turnaround time, often to below one day per loaded journey in some districts of the North Eastern Region and thus the envy of other parts of the country.

BR – A Very Early User of Computers in Britain

As early as 1959, BR installed in the Physics Division of their Research Department, Derby an electronic digital computer, which was unique in the country. An Elliott 402F computer, it was one of only two such machines in Europe. It was a general purpose, automatic, binary computer, designed primarily to tackle scientific and engineering problems in which the mathematics were either too complex, or too lengthy to be performed by desk machines. Its use also considerably reduced the time taken in the comparatively straightforward work which was a feature of research. The computer had a medium-sized memory enabling it to store and perform operations on over 4,000 numbers simultaneously, the input and output of data being by paper tape. An additional feature of the machine was that floating point arithmetic could be used thus permitting greater accuracy in a far bigger range of numbers. The speed of the computer was that pairs of numbers, each of nine digits, could be multiplied at the rate of 300 in one second.

The machine was used to make calculations on vibration problems, such as those concerned with the improvement of passenger coach comfort, the analysis of stresses in structures and bridges, and problems relating to the development of continuous braking for freight trains. A further field was that of statistical enquiries, such as determining optimum conditions where many variable factors were concerned – for example, the most economic means of carrying out a complex set of wagon movements.

Bringing Home the Milk

From the early days of railways, trains were used to transport milk to large cities. Initially it was carried in churns and deft porters were able to trundle two along, one in each hand. The 17-gallon churns weighed 2¼ cwts when full. Many rural stations dealt with milk traffic.

The dairy at Wootton Bassett, just west of Swindon, was the first in England to use bulk milk tanks. Tanks were much more economical than churns. One man could rinse a tank with cold water and scrub it, gaining access through a manhole. It was then rinsed with hot water and finally sterilised with steam, a much easier operation than carrying out all these procedures with 176 17-gallon churns which held the equivalent of one tank. Furthermore, the 176 churns needed three vans to carry them and weighed a total of 80 tons, whereas one tank only weighed 22 tons.

The 3,000 gallon enamel glass-lined tanks were manufactured by the Dairy Supply Company and the chassis built at Swindon. The dairy owned the actual tank, while the GWR owned and maintained the underframe. Each tank was insulated with a 2 inch layer of cork, which meant that the milk left the factory at 38 degrees Fahrenheit and the temperature rose by no more than one degree on its journey to Willesden. The service was inaugurated on 1 December 1927.

The Vinegar Branch

Worcester had a fascinating 900 yards long, steeply-graded branch. Opened in 1872 it carried 5,000 tons of vinegar annually. As it was on a gradient, to guard against runaways when shunting sidings, a brake van was always required to be stationed at the lower end of the vehicles as breakaways over busy level crossings could have had particularly serious consequences.

Road traffic was warned by a railway signal and the crossing keeper equipped with flags, stopped all traffic, including pedestrians, over the crossing by exhibiting a red flag until the train had passed. He exhibited a green flag to the engine driver as an indication that road traffic had been stopped and that the train could proceed. At night hand-lamps were used.

At the vinegar works at the lower end of the branch, wagons were run in by gravitation and it was essential that the brake van was the leading vehicle owing to lack of clearance for staff to apply brakes to the moving vehicles. The line was last used on 5 June 1964.

Hop-Pickers' Specials

In the nineteenth and the first part of the twentieth century, hop-pickers' specials were a great feature. In 1893 so many hop-pickers arrived on the Down platform at Tonbridge that they overflowed on to the tracks and the stationmaster refused to permit the entry of another hop-pickers' train. This greatly annoyed some of the more boisterous elements of the crowd that they attempted to burn down the waiting room and order was only restored after mounted police charged along the Down platform and made several arrests. Until the First World War, a special hand-cart was kept at Tonbridge police station to trundle any hop-pickers to the cells if the officer at the station ticket barrier considered them unfit to travel.

Most of the hop-pickers arrived in special trains, the rolling stock often extremely antiquated with paint peeling off and much of the upholstery tattered or very thin, and a ride in such a train, apart from the hearty company, was certainly an interesting experience.

The Railway Strike of 1911

The most extensive paralysis of transport in Britain up to that time occurred in August 1911. It arose as a result of widespread labour unrest, culminating in a national railway strike.

It started with a stoppage at the London Docks which threatened food supplies and caused three-quarters of London bus services to be suspended due to a lack of petrol. Railwaymen at Liverpool and Manchester then became involved and a widespread strike appeared imminent.

The government offered to place at the service of the railway companies 'every available soldier in the country.' This was solely to protect property and maintain public order, but the action was widely interpreted otherwise.

A general railway strike began on 18 August. The military was called out to guard focal points such as signal boxes, locomotive depots, tunnels and main line stations. The full-dress headgear worn by the Guards, with khaki field uniform caused soldiers to suffer considerably in the hundred degree Fahrenheit temperature in the height of an exceptionally hot summer.

G. W. R.

PASSENGER TRAIN SERVICE

In consequence of Labour Troubles,

it is regretted that it is not possible to continue the whole of the advertised Passenger Train Services.

It is hoped that a considerable number of the Company's staff will remain loyal and at work, and the greatest care will be taken to avoid unnecessary inconvenience and delay to passengers, mails and perishable traffic.

A special pamphlet is issued, and is obtainable at the stations, setting out particulars of the train service it is intended, if practicable, to run for the conveyance of passengers.

OTHER TRAINS USUALLY RUN WILL BE TEMPORARILY CANCELLED.

Through carriages ordinarily run to and from certain stations will be discontinued, and passengers may be required to change at junctions en route.

Restaurant, Dining and Sleeping Cars will be discontinued. Refreshments may be obtained at the principal stations.

All Excursion Trains and Cheap Fare Arrangements will be temporarily suspended.

Horse and Carriage, Motor Car and similar traffic will not be accepted for conveyance by rail.

The usual arrangements for the through booking of passengers to other Companies' lines will be subject to variation, and connections with other Companies' trains cannot be guaranteed.

The Company will not be able to convey unlimited numbers of passengers by the trains which will be run, and if passengers cannot be provided with accommodation by any particular train they must travel by subsequent trains.

The Company also give notice that they are unable to guarantee the punctuality of trains, and cannot be responsible for any delay, loss or damage to passenger train traffic.

JAMES C. INGLIS, General Manager.

103. GWR poster published in connection with the railway strike of 1911.

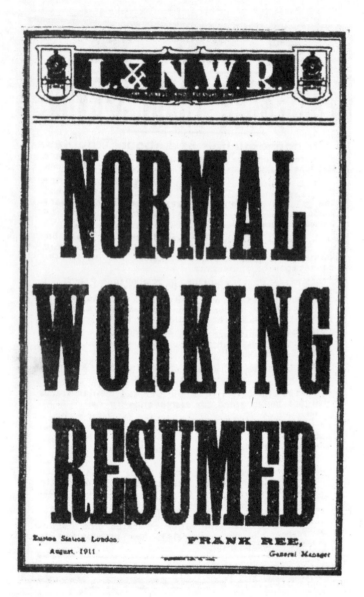

104. London & North Western Railway poster published following the settlement of the railway strike of 1911.

At a meeting held under the auspices of the President of the Board of Trade, a compromise was reached on 19 August and a Royal Commission appointed. The outcome was generally regarded as a victory for the trade unions, and Mr Lloyd George said that the government had effected a settlement of 'one of the most menacing industrial strikes with which this country had ever been confronted.'

Bovril Advertisements

In the first half of the twentieth century Messrs Bovril used clever and ingenious railway-themed phrases to advertise their products on stations. Examples being:

He'd rather Mrs Train than Mrs Bovril.
If you've Mr Train, don't Miss Bovril.
Tour better than one – if they're Bovril sandwiches.
The engine was coaled – so they gave it Bovril.
What made the boiler fitter? Daily Bovril.
Guards flag – if they miss their Daily Bovril.
If you train on Bovril you won't miss your train.
Tickets please! So do Bovril sandwiches.
Bovril makes ordinary fare first class.
All change until they try Bovril.
If you can't go by train go buy Bovril.
The fastest train on Bovril.
The Scotch Express great faith in Bovril.
You will never find Bovril in the lost property office.
For every season Bovril is the ticket.
2.40fy take Bovril.
Bovril the goods for passengers.
Bovril brightens up old buffers.
Faulty sleepers need Bovril.
A daily Bovril is cheaper than a weakly season.

Use Your Loaf

When the London & South Western Railway electrified some of its London suburban lines, headcodes were carried and shown by black stencils over an opal plate at the front of the new electric trains, with the blank opal of the rear motor coach acting as a last vehicle indication. The letters gave a clue to the service: East Putney to Wimbledon was P; the roundabout V; Shepperton S; Hampton Court H; Hounslow Loop O and Claygate, rather illogically, I.

A certain flour miller's imaginative publicity department spotted that the letters could form 'HOVIS'!

The Severn Tunnel

The Severn tunnel had quite a number of peculiarities. Some of the houses built at Sudbrook for the workmen were built of concrete – a very early example of this use of the material.

On the east bank of the Severn, due to the difficulty experienced in obtaining land, wooden houses were built over the line of the tunnel, timber being lighter and less likely to cause settlement.

One night a brick chimney between two houses collapsed straight down into the ground. The next morning it was amazing to hear of all the trousers and waistcoats containing money and watches which had been hung on nails driven into that chimney!

The Great Spring flooded the tunnel workings and it was believed that before pumping operations could begin, an iron door in a headwall which had been left open by panic-stricken men, needed to be closed. After several attempts, a diver reached the door and turned the valve the number of times he was told would close it. Pumps were started and the water level gradually sank. When the heading was finally pumped clear, the foreman walked up the heading and discovered the cause of the slowness – the valve had a left-hand screw and was in fact closed when the diver reached it and had, in fact, turned it open!

A Road Tunnel Becomes a Railway Tunnel

Between 1825 and 1843 Marc and Isambard Brunel constructed a tunnel under the Thames. Originally it was intended to be for vehicular use and its dimensions allowed a hay cart to pass through. Shortage of cash meant that the sloping ramps had to be omitted and replaced with ninety-nine steps so it was only of use to pedestrians. To increase revenue the tunnel was turned into the world's first underwater shopping mall and did a good trade selling souvenirs. It was not until 1865 when the tunnel was purchased by the East London Railway that its cost proved justified.

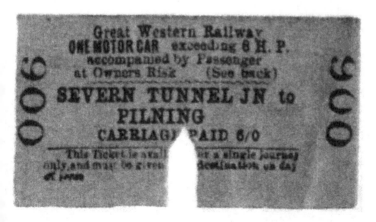

105. Before the opening of the Severn road bridge in 1966, the Severn Tunnel provided a shortcut for cars between England and Wales. This ticket issued in 1937 was for the transport of a car between Severn Tunnel Junction and Pilning. It cost six shillings.

106. Cutting the Severn Tunnel.

The East London Railway ran from the Great Eastern Railway's terminus at Liverpool Street to New Cross to connect with the London, Brighton & South Coast Railway and also the South Eastern Railway. In 1913 the line was electrified.

Going the Long Way Round

It is rare that a train takes the wrong turning, but this happened early in the SR days. A Tonbridge line peak-hour train, due to call first at Chislehurst, was diverted south of London Bridge to the Brighton line by an errant signalman. The driver, equally sleepy, failed to notice the odd route and obeyed what had been set up.

Having crossed to the Brighton side of the twelve-track main line out of London Bridge, it was impossible to turn back and the only sensible solution was to continue to Tonbridge via Redhill, reverse and then call at the intended stops in the reverse order, finishing at Chislehurst after a 60-mile diversion – instead of the normal 10-mile trip.

A Shipping Mishap

Most of the principal railway companies had shipping interests, as indeed did some of the smaller ones, even the Weston, Clevedon & Portishead Light Railway possessed its own wharf and vessel.

One ship owned by the London & South Western Railway was the *Lorina*, launched in 1918 by Lady Walker, wife of Sir Herbert Walker, general manager of the company. She named it after herself.

The story, probably apocryphal, went round the head offices of the LSWR at Waterloo, that one morning a message appeared on Sir Herbert's desk: 'Lorina on the rocks outside Jersey with a hole in her bottom making water fast.'

Highest Altitude on British Railways

Height above Sea Level	Railway	Summit	Route
3,140	Snowdon	Snowdon	
1,484	LMS	Drumochter	Perth–Aviemore
1,474	LNER	Parkhead	Burnhill–Stanhope
1,405	LMS	Leadhills	Elvanfoot–Wanlockhead
1,400	LMS	Waen Avon	Bryn Mawr–Pontypool
1,378	LNER	Weatherill	
1,373	GWR	Princetown	Yelverton–Princetown
1,370	LNER	Bloweth	Battersby–Rosedale
1,369	LNER	Stainmore	Darlington–Kirkby Stephen
1,350	LNER	Corrour	Crianlarich–Fort William
1,315	LMS	Slochd Mhuic	Aviemore–Inverness

Longest British Railway Tunnels

Name	Railway	Stations between	Length (miles)	Length (yards)
Severn	GWR	Pilning–Severn Tunnel Jc	4	624
Totley	LMS	Dore–Grindleford	3	950
Standedge	LMS	Marsden–Diggle	3	57
Woodhead	LNER	Woodhead–Dunford Bridge	3	13
Sodbury	GWR	Badminton–Chipping Sodbury	2	913
Disley	LMS	Chinley–Cheadle Heath	2	346
Bramhope	LNER	Horsforth–Arthington	2	234

Festiniog	LMS	Roman Bridge–Festiniog	2	206
Cowburn	LMS	Edale–Chinley	2	102
Sevenoaks	SR	Sevenoaks–Hildenborough	1	1691

The LMS Standedge Tunnel between Manchester and Leeds had two unique claims to distinction. One was that three parallel tunnels were driven for a length of over 3 miles: one carrying double track while the other two each accommodating a single track, thus making four roads in total.

The second claim to distinction is that it is the only railway tunnel in the world in which track water troughs were laid. This unique location was determined by the fact that it was the only appreciable length of level track between Manchester and Leeds.

Longest Daily Non-Stop Railway Runs in Great Britain in 1928

Railway	Between	Distance (miles)	Av. Spd (mph)	Name of Train
LNER	King's Cross–Edinburgh	392.7	47.6	*Flying Scotsman*
LMS	Euston–Carlisle	300.8	52.0	*Royal Scot*
LMS	Carlisle–Euston	298.2	50.7	*Royal Scot*
LMS	Glasgow–Crewe	243.2	45.6	*Night Scot*
GWR	Paddington–Plymouth	225.7	56.4	*Cornish Riviera*
LMS	Euston–Prestatyn	205.5	51.8	*The Welshman*
GWR	Paddington–Torquay	199.7	57.1	*Torbay Limited*
GWR	Newton Abbot–Paddington	193.9	56.8	*Torbay Limited*
LMS	Euston–Liverpool	189.7	55.3	*London–Merseyside Express*
LNER	King's Cross–York	188.2	53.8	*Scarborough Flyer*

Fastest Daily Runs in Great Britain in 1928

Railway	Between	Distance	Average speed
GWR	Swindon–Paddington	77.3	61.8
GWR	Paddington–Bath	106.9	61.6
LNER	Darlington–York	44.1	61.5
LNER	Leicester–Nottingham	22.6	61.5
GWR	Paddington–Westbury	95.6	61.0
GWR	Paddington–Exeter	173.7	60.2
LNER	Aylesbury–Leicester	65.1	60.1
GWR	Kemble–Paddington	91.0	60.0
LNER	Brackley–Rugby	23.9	59.8
GWR	High Wycombe–Leamington	60.8	59.8

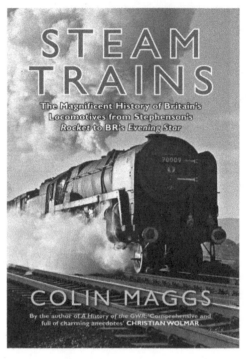